21

O.U.T. Spells Out

David Holman

Introduction and Activities by Lawrence Till

Series editor: Lawrence Till

Heinemann Educational Publishers
Halley Court, Jordan Hill, Oxford OX2 8EJ
a division of Reed Educational & Professional Publishing Ltd

OXFORD   MELBOURNE   AUCKLAND
JOHANNESBURG   BLANTYRE   GABORONE
IBADAN   PORTSMOUTH (NH) USA   CHICAGO

Play copyright © David Holman 1998
Introduction and activities copyright © Lawrence Till 1998

First published in the Heinemann Plays series 1998

2002 2001 2000 99 98

10 9 8 7 6 5 4 3 2

Acknowledgements
With thanks to the original cast and all involved in the first performance of this play by the
Blackpool Grand Theatre in 1997, directed by Deborah Yhip.

CAUTION
This play is fully protected by copyright. Any enquiries concerning the rights for
professional or amateur stage production should be addressed to David Holman,
48 Castlewood Road, London N16 6DW

ISBN 0 435 23323 8

Original design by Jeffrey White Creative Associates; adapted by Jim Turner
Typeset by 🛧 Tek-Art, Croydon, Surrey
Cover illustration by Rob Hefferan
Cover design by Aricot Vert
Printed and bound in the United Kingdom by Clays Ltd, St Ives plc

CONTENTS

INTRODUCTION

O.U.T. Spells Out is a play by David Holman inspired by Margaret Humphreys' marvellous and moving book *Empty Cradles*. The book tells of the exportation of unwanted children from post-war Britain to various countries of the then Empire, under the so-called 'Child Migration Scheme'. There had been forcible exportation of children from these Islands since 1618 but this practice accelerated in the period after the War. By 1967, when the Child Migration Scheme ended, 150,000 children had been sent away to different parts of the British Empire, including Australia, Canada, New Zealand, and to a lesser extent, South Africa, Southern Rhodesia (now Zimbabwe) and the Caribbean.

Most of the children were selected for emigration because it was thought that they were at risk in some way – perhaps of being badly treated by their families. Some had been placed in homes. Some parents with family problems couldn't cope and handed over their children to various children's homes or agencies which then sent them overseas either with or without their parents' knowledge. The vast majority of children were sent without their parents' knowledge and consent. Children were frequently told that they were orphans who had neither parent alive in Britain. Brothers and sisters and even twins were separated as a result of these schemes. Few children were prepared for their new lives abroad or understood why they were sent overseas. Many were not given copies of their birth certificates or any details about their family background.

Margaret Humphreys is the Director and Founder of the Child Migrants Trust, an organization working on behalf of former child migrants who seek information about their childhood and family history, and those anxious to be reunited with their mothers, fathers, brothers or sisters. She comments: 'Over the past ten years, my colleagues and I have spent many hours in television and radio stations in order to bring the plight of Britain's child migrants before a wider audience. We have co-operated with dozens of journalists in Britain and overseas so that newspapers and magazines could tell the story of the courage and pain as well as the joys and heartaches of this remarkable group of people.'

The play was first presented by Blackpool Grand Youth Theatre in March 1997. David Holman comments:

Writing a play for a youth theatre, the last thing one wants is for the performers to have to play middle-aged characters. So I decided to try and tell the story through the discovery by today's children of these appalling events of our recent history, children discovering a children's story.

O.U.T. Spells Out is a moving play about a serious and tragic episode in our recent past.

Lawrence Till

ABOUT THE AUTHOR

David Holman has written more than 70 works for stage, radio, film and opera which have been performed for or by children. His work has been translated into many languages and has been produced on every continent.

As with this play, his work habitually has a strong social and political dimension. *Drink the Mercury* (1972) dealt with the effects of heavy metal pollution on the fishermen of Minamata in Japan, *The Disappeared* (1979) with military repression in Latin America, *Solomon's Cat* (1987) about wildlife poaching in East Africa, and *Whale* (1989) with the rescue of three grey whales in Alaska by a combination of US and Russian personnel at a time when the two superpowers were divided by the 'Cold War'.

Other plays by David Holman in Heinemann Plays:

Whale
Solomon's Cat
A Christmas Carol (Adaptation)

FROM DAVID HOLMAN

This play is an attempt to tell the story of thousands of British children, some orphans but many not, who in the years following the Second World War were shipped to the countries of the British Empire – and a new life. The children had been promised that there was a warm welcome waiting for them in New Zealand, Canada, Southern Rhodesia (now Zimbabwe) and Australia. They were promised that families in those countries wanted to adopt them, love them and bring them up.

The reality was, in most cases, very different. Often the children were treated as virtual slaves by farmers and shop-keepers who wanted unpaid child labour. Those who asked about brothers or sisters back in England were often told that the brothers and sisters had died – when they hadn't. Even today, these former child migrants (who are now perhaps sixty or seventy years old) are finding relatives – mothers, fathers, sisters and brothers – whom they had believed all their adult lives to be dead.

With such great numbers of children involved, you would think that the facts about this mass migration would be widely known, but until recently almost nobody knew about it. It was a dark history and the worse for being virtually secret. It is largely due to the work of one woman that this scandalous episode in our recent history has been uncovered. Margaret Humphreys was a Nottingham social worker. In the course of her work she met a woman who started to remember that, as a tiny child, she had had a brother. She began to remember some people arriving to take the little brother away somewhere. At first Mrs Humphreys couldn't believe that such a thing was possible. As she began to investigate, it became clear that many more children than this brother had indeed been taken away and then sent halfway across the world. The authorities in both Australia and Britain made it very difficult for anyone to trace these migrant children. With great resolution (and with the support of Nottingham Council) Mrs Humphreys set up an organization which managed to reunite many ex-migrants with their relatives, and it is still doing so. This story is told in her marvellous book, *Empty Cradles*, without which this play couldn't have been written.

David Holman

LIST OF CHARACTERS

Characters for 'today'

Old Billy (Simmons)
*Survivor of war
and migration, looking
for his sister*

Elizabeth Carter
Charlie Carter
*Sister and brother:
orphans, new to
their school*

Steve O'Neill
Australian backpacker

Gerry Higgins
Millie Church
Council site workers

Paramedic 1
Paramedic 2

Child 1
Child 2
Child 3

Security Guard

Students

Sandy Correy
Donna Jones
Marcia Stone
Eva Jupp
Darlene Hemmings
Tricia Gunn
Steve Willis
Mark Marshall
Darren Andrews
Thomas Swift

Characters for 1940s–50s

Billy Simmons
Alice Simmons
*Brother and sister,
separated following
Second World War*

Billy and Alice's mother
Young adult 1
Young adult 2
Sailor
Airman

Soldier

Voice
(air raid warden)

Chant
Recorded voice
P.C. Wilson

Noel Roche
Murray Roche
Australian farm boys

Wartime Children (The Gang)

Freddie Hill	Wartime child 1
Brian Batson	Wartime child 2
Trevor Ford	Wartime child 3

Migrant children

Carole Brine/Thin girl	Trevor Wymark
Jennie Richardson	Philip Sims
Nan Brookes	David Steen
Maria Santorini	Henry Smith
Barbara Court	Christopher Morris
Betty French	Alex Young
May Scott	Brian York

Staff and crew

Miss Starkey

Meg Kelly
Ronnie Howard
Stewards

Monks and Nuns

Brother James
Brother Simon
Brother Michael
Brother John
Sister Mary
Two nuns *(non-speaking)*

ACT ONE

Scene 1

School playground, today. Music. In the dark, a recorded chant.

Chant   O-U-T spells out, so out you must go,
Because the King and Queen say so.
(Repeat twice.)

*The sound of a large noisy school. Present day.
Lights up on the stage as three teenage Students,
Sandy Correy, Donna Jones and Marcia Stone, walk
across chattering and laughing in school uniform.
Their uniform is distinctive (say red). We see a sign
reading 'Danger' next to a canvased-off digging site
where Gerry Higgins and Millie Church are working.
There is a wheelbarrow with a couple of spades, etc.
A young backpacker, Steve O'Neill, appears at the
other side. We see a big Australian flag on the flap
of his backpack. He is holding a local map guide.*

Steve O'Neill   Excuse me. Am I right for Addison Road? I'm lost.
The Students giggle.
Steve O'Neill   Looking for a place called 'Sunnyview.' A big house.
Sandy   There's no 'Sunnyview' on Addison Road. I deliver
papers up there. . . no, I'm sure. Sunnyview?
Anyway, Addison Road's that way. Two traffic lights,
then left.

Steve O'Neill   Aw, thanks. G'day.

Students   *(giggling)* G'day – mate.

The Students chat as they watch him go. Behind them, a young workman, Gerry, comes up out of the hole and jumps the barrier. He wears overalls with 'Council' on the back.The Students turn and wolf-whistle at him.

Donna   Check the muscles.

Gerry   *(smiling)* Behave yourselves.

They whistle again.

Gerry   Go on. Harassing poor innocent workmen in the course of their duties.

Marcia   Found anything down there?

Gerry   You'll be the first to know.

Sandy   Why did the playground collapse?

Gerry   It's a mystery. Shouldn't you be at your lessons?

Marcia   See you at break!

The Students start moving off. Lights on the school fence, where a middle-aged man, Old Billy, is standing with a suitcase at his feet.

Old Billy   *(grasping the wire)* Alice!!

Sandy   Oh no, not him again.

Marcia   He's harmless. Some old care-in-the-community nutter.

Sandy   Yeah, but he's been there hours now. *(Shouts)* Here! Nutter! There's no Alice at this school. You're in the wrong place. All right?

Old Billy   Alice!!

Students   *(mockingly as they exit)* Alice!!

Marcia   *(bending down to tie her shoes)* Wait. Wait!

They don't wait and Marcia is left behind.

Scene 2

Same time, same place. Millie's hand, in which there is a Second World War helmet, appears above the canvas of the digging site. Marcia goes across to look.

Millie *(unseen)* Gerry!

Gerry *(taking the helmet)* Hmmm!

Gerry puts the helmet on.

Marcia *(looking at the helmet)* Here. Can I go show that to my friends Darlene and Tricia? They did a big project on the war and that round here. *(Marcia holds her hand out.)* Go on.

Gerry shakes his head. He is being awkward.

Marcia Oh!

Marcia turns to look down the hole as a very small boy, Charlie Carter in (say) blue uniform, wanders on. He has a piece of paper in his hand and is lost. He turns it upside down. He sees Gerry.

Charlie Room 10, Mister?

Gerry I'm a stranger here myself, young man.

Charlie *(of the helmet)* Where did you get that?

Gerry indicates the hole and Charlie looks down into it.

Gerry Either I've gone colourblind or you're at the wrong school.

Charlie *(of the uniform)* This is my old school's. First day. Any bombs down there?

Gerry *(checking map)* I hope not.

Charlie *(of the helmet)* Can I try it on?

Gerry *(giving it to him)* Yes, but keep away from this.

Millie appears with a spade.

Millie   We'll need an older map. It looks like there's the
              remains of a street under here. They must have built
              the school on top of it.

Marcia   Listen, I told you!! *(She holds out her hand for the
              helmet.)* Darlene and Tricia have got old maps. And
              photos. It's all in the library. Do I go and get 'em for
              you?

              *Gerry nods, takes the helmet from Charlie and gives
              it to Marcia.*

Charlie   *(disappointed)* Ohh!

              Charlie and Marcia go into the school.

Scene 3

*Later that morning. Same place. The bell goes for
break.*

Gerry   Millie, back to the van. I'm not working while that
              horde of savages is out for its break. Cup of tea.
              (Calls across to Charlie, who appears at a doorway.)
              Guard that hole, young man.

              *Millie and Gerry start to exit as a large group of
              Students noisily start to enter the playground. The
              Girls in the group wolf-whistle at Gerry.*

Gerry   Behave!

              *A group of Boys, Mark Marshall, Darren Andrews
              and Steve Willis, start tossing a ball around.*

Mark   *(of the canvas and debris in the playground)*
              How're we supposed to have a game with all this?
              (He takes kick at the debris.) Right. Charlotte
              Hornets this end. Krauts that end.

Darren   Pass.

              Old Billy continues to call through the fence.

Old Billy Alice!!

Mark	Him again! He's doing my head in.
Charlie	Is he a prowler?
Steve Willis	Prowler? He's just some old fruitcake.
Mark	*(mocking)* Alice!!
Eva	Leave him alone.
Steve Willis	*(shouts to Old Billy)* Read my lips. There. . . is. . . no . . . Alice.

Charlie has wandered from the hole and into the middle of the basketball game. Mark Marshall stops playing with the ball and looks at him.

Darren	Mark – pass!

Mark waits.

Darren	Pass!
Mark	(to Charlie) You!
Charlie	Eh?
Mark	What do you think you're doing?
Eva	Marshall!
Charlie	Nothing.
Mark	This is my court.
Charlie	Sorry.
Eva	Leave him alone, Marshall. He's new. He hasn't had the chance to discover what a king-size prat you are.
Mark	Kiss!
Charlie	Uh?
Mark	On your knees. Kiss my court.
Darren	Mark, let's get on with the game.
Mark	Now!
Darren	We've only got a couple of minutes.

Charlie starts to get down.

Eva	Marshall!

Charlie is almost on the floor with Mark standing over him. The voice of Elizabeth Carter is heard offstage.

Voice   You!

An older teenager, also dressed in blue uniform, strides in. This is Elizabeth.

Elizabeth   Charlie. What the – Up!

Darren   Another one! Where're they all coming from?

Elizabeth   *(to Mark)* I'll say this once, whatever your name is. That's my brother. You touch him again – ever – and I'll punch your teeth so far down your throat you'll be brushing your teeth through your underpants. All right?

Everyone is amazed. They wait to see if Mark will make a move. He doesn't.

Elizabeth   All right?

Cheers from the watching Students as they see that Mark is not moving. Now he has to do something.

Mark   You and whose army?

Elizabeth   No army. Just me.

Elizabeth stands right up against him threateningly. He doesn't move.

Marcia   Marshall, there – bottom of your trousers – is that liquid?

Sandy   No. He always wears brown socks.

Marcia/Sandy   *(hilarious laughter)* Ahahahaha.

Elizabeth turns away to Charlie. The angry Mark grabs a spade from the barrow. Gerry comes back and smoothly takes it out of his hand.

Gerry   Council property, son. On your bike.

Darren   Come on, let's have a game! Bell'll be going.

Mark angrily grabs the ball and flings it hard at Darren. They play.

Mark   *(to Charlie)* I'll have you.

Girls delight in the discomfiture of Mark.

Elizabeth   Charlie, we're going to get your stuff in a minute. We're not staying here.

Charlie	But, Sis!
Elizabeth	I don't like the people here.
	Gerry approaches from backstage.
Gerry	*(to Elizabeth)* Nice one.
Elizabeth	What?
Gerry	That moron. I saw you from the van.
Elizabeth	*(nods a smile)* Charlie, run and ask that old fella what he wants.
Charlie	Sis?? He looks nutty.
	Elizabeth indicates for Charlie to go without argument. He shrugs and wanders off.
Gerry	You don't like this place?
Elizabeth	No, we'll try somewhere else.
Gerry	What will your Dad and Mum say?
Elizabeth	Haven't got any. It's just me and him. I decide.

Scene 4

Same time, same place. Marcia enters the playground with two girls, Darlene Hemmings and Tricia Gunn. They have maps, folders and photos.

Marcia	Found 'em. *(Hands Gerry a map and turns to Elizabeth.)* 'Bout time someone gave Marshall what for. I saw it from up there. Excellent. These two were in the library as usual. The swots.
	All look at the documents as Charlie arrives back.
Charlie	*(indicating)* His name's Billy Simmons and he wants to find his sister. And he says what's this school doing here? His street should be here.
Darlene	His street? *(Shows map.)* There hasn't been a street here for forty years.

Charlie has now managed to get the helmet and looks at it carefully while the dialogue continues.

Marcia   *(of Old Billy)* He is a nutter.

Tricia   Wait a minute. Wait a minute. Wait a minute. Alice and Billy Simmons? They're in one of these photos. A kids' party to celebrate the end of the war. Names on the back. That's him.

They look over from the photo to him.

Darlene   *(demonstrates)* That photo was taken *(Positions herself)* right here. See, the street was here. *(Points)* Pub. *(Points again)* Sweet shop. *(Points again)* Underground air raid shelter for the kids.

Tricia   This side of the street was bombed flat in the war. More or less an accident – the German planes were supposed to be bombing the docks. *(Points)* They flew in that way.

Charlie   *(shows the helmet)* Initials. A.S.

Elizabeth   Alice Simmons?

The bell goes for the end of break.

Tricia   Listen. What about we see you here after school?

Gerry   She won't be here. She's leaving.

**Marcia/Tricia/
Darlene**   What?

The Students are all starting to head into the school.

Elizabeth   We're not leaving just yet.

Darlene   *(going)* Stay. We need someone to squash Marshall. You know – like pest control.

Elizabeth and Charlie are left alone with some of the folders.

Charlie   *(taking a newspaper)* Here's something. 'The Evening Chronicle'. 'The Night We Were Bombed'.

Elizabeth takes it with interest and they read.

Music. A very young girl, Alice Simmons, in wartime clothes and wearing a large helmet, skips across the stage. Old Billy grasps at the fence. He looks up.

Old Billy   Alice!!

She skips some more. We hear the sound of the bombers. Voice of Billy as a young child.

Billy   Alice!!

Scene 5

Albion Street in the Second World War. Lighting change and then the louder sound of bombers.

Alice   *(looking around but not seeing anything)* Billy!

Billy's voice   Alice! Get below ground. They're coming. Bombers!

**Elizabeth/
Charlie**   *(looking around).* What is happening?

They look up as if they see the planes circling above. Sound of air raid warning. They cover their ears.

Megaphone shout.

Voice   Don't panic, children. Go calmly to the air raid shelter. Don't forget your gas masks and your tin hats.

Shadowy figures race across the stage. Some in shorts. Ragged.

Freddie   Mum!! Mum!! Where are you.

Billy   *(cricket bat in hand)* Alice!! Alice!!

Voice   Into the shelters.

Freddie   Mum!! Where are you, Mum??

Billy   Bombs!! Get down!!!

Then the sound of the bombs falling. All the figures have flung themselves down in the dark.

Billy   Alice!! Alice!!

Alice   Billy! Billy!

Then brief silence. The sound of fire engines in the distance and the stage fills with the Kids of Albion Street and two Firefighters with a hose. Running in all directions. Some with buckets.

Trevor Ford That way, Mister! Albion St!

Billy   Alice!

Trevor Ford Quick!!

Freddie   That's our house. Mum!!

Billy   Alice!

Alice   *(appearing)* Billy! Billy!

Billy   Alice, where were you?

Alice   I couldn't get to the shelter.

Billy   Why not? I was worried sick.

Alice   Wing of a German plane. It blocked the road. There's some children killed. Where's Mum?

Billy   In the shelter. She's looking after what'shername.

Trevor Ford *(as Kids gather)* Billy – coming to see that German plane? Pilot might still be alive.

Billy   No. Better wait for Mum.

Sound of ack ack. All the Kids look up to the sky.

Billy   Look – the Germans are running.

Trevor Ford *(picking up a piece of stick)* Well, I'm going.

Alice   Billy, is our dad up there shooting at the Germans?

Billy   He's not a pilot. Anyway, he's in Africa. Why don't you listen?

Trevor Ford *(to the sky)* You missed, you bleeders. You'll never get us.

Billy   You'll never beat the English.

Trevor Ford England. England.

Billy   You missed.

All Children   You missed.
You tried to bomb our heads in and
You missed.
You loaded your bombs in Germany
And think to yourself along the way
We'll get those English kids today
Buttttttttttttttttttttttttttttttttttt. . .
You missed.
I'm sorry, Mr Hitler, but you missed.
Your bombers fly in to attack
But we just fart, the bombs fly back,
And we're still here and that's a fact.
You missed
You missed.
Sorry, Mr Hitler, but you missed.
(*softer*) Sorry, Mr Hitler, but you missed.
(*even softer*) Sorry, Mr Hitler, but you missed.

Laughter.

Alice   Three cheers for the Albion Street kids!

All   Hurrah. Hurrah. Hurrah. Salt, mustard, vinegar,
pepper.

*They go briefly into skipping game with the refrain
being chanted by all.*

Scene 6

*Time passes. Same place, May 1945. Albion Street
Kids are playing the skipping game. A small girl,
Carole Brine, enters and interrupts the game.*

Carole   Hey! Everyone. Heard the news?

All   What news?

Carole   War's over. They're coming home. They're coming
home.

All Hurrah!! Salt, mustard, vinegar, pepper.

Time passes. Six months later. They chant and skip. Then the sound of marching steps. A couple of Wartime Children take small union jacks from pockets and wave them wildly and cheer.

Children Hurrah! Salt, mustard, vinegar, pepper.

The Wartime Children move to the front stage.

Child 1 Here they come!!

Child 2 Look – the Tommies!

Child 3 Dad! Dad!

Child 1 Are any of them your Dad, Billy?

Billy Dunno what he looks like now.

Child 2 Look, the Navy! The Navy!

Child 3 Dad! Dad!! Here, it's me!! What's he walking away for? Oh no, that can't be him.

Child 1 Where is he? Where is he?

Child 2 Here come the Air Force!

Child 3 My Dad's a flier.

Child 1 Flier? Your Dad's ground crew. He just mends the planes for 'em.

Child 3 So??

Child 1 They couldn't have won the war without my Dad. Dad! That can't be him.

A Sailor, an Airman and a Soldier arrive at the rear with their kit bags. All the Wartime Children turn, including Alice and Billy.

Child 2 Dad! Dad! Here! Here!

The three young Servicemen (some wounded) put the bags down and put their arms out in front of them. The Wartime Children put their arms out hopefully.

Child 3 Dad! Dad!

The Servicemen come forward to the Wartime Children. They alight on their children, lift them into the air and swing them around as the less lucky ones watch. Great joy for the lucky Children.

Children 1–3   Hurrah!

The lucky Wartime Children are carried or led off. The music and marching sound dies. Billy and Alice plus Carole are left on the stage.

Scene 7

Same time, same place. Billy and Alice plus Carole muse and kick their heels disappointedly some distance from each other.

Billy   They can't all come back at once. Maybe there's Germans left over need killing. When my Dad comes back he's taking us to the seaside. We're getting a bucket and spade.

Carole   Huh! MINE's taking us to 'Merica.

Billy   A Yank?? You'll be lucky. The Yanks are gone. They're gone.

Carole   No! My Dad hasn't gone, anyway.

Billy   It was on the radio. Here, and I bet he didn't marry your Mum, did he? They never do, Yanks.

Carole   They do! Mum couldn't have had me if she wasn't married. Clever!

Billy   What's your name?

Carole   Not telling you!! Carole Brine. What's yours?

The Gang   *(entering)* Billy Simmons. Billy Simmons. Billy Simmons.

The Gang of Wartime Children come and make a menacing walking circle around Billy.

The Gang   *(pointing at him threateningly)*

O-U-T spells out, and out you must go
Because the King and Queen say so.
(Repeat)
Billy puts his fists up as they circle him.

Billy   Get lost. What do you want?

Freddie   Want to hear the latest?

Billy   No. Buzz off.

Freddie   Well, you're gonna. Yeah, 'cause guess what? Your Dad's dead. Your Dad's dead.

The Gang   Dead dad. Dead dad. Dead dad.

Alice   No, he's not! He's not!

The Gang   Yes, he is!

Alice   No, he's not!

The Gang   He is! He is! He is! You ain't got a dad! Hahahahaha!

Carole   Leave them alone! You don't know their Dad's dead. They wouldn't tell you.

Brian   My brother knows because he delivers the telegrams, see.

Carole   Leave them alone.

Freddie   Ohh, look who you've got sticking up for you, Billy. Her Mum's got three kids from Yankee soldiers. *(Chants)* Unmarried mother.

The Gang   Unmarried mother. Unmarried mother.

Carole   Shut up! Shut up! You can't have babies if you're not married. So there!!

Freddie   Oh yeah? So where's your Dad then?

Carole   He's taking us to 'Merica.

Child 3   America? They've all gone home.

Billy   Leave her alone.

The Gang   Dead dad! Dead dad!

Billy   Come here and say that.

Freddie   And guess what? Your Mum can't look after you.

No one'll give her a job with two kids if they know she's on her own. So guess what – she's putting you in a home.

The Gang Children's home! Children's home! Children's home!

Billy No, she's not! She's not putting us in a home. She's not!!

Billy flings himself at Freddie. They fight and kick and punch with The Gang egging them on.

The Gang O-U-T spells out, so out you must go!

Carole Get him, Billy!!

The Gang Kick him, Freddie.

Alice Strangle him, Billy!!

The Gang Give him what for, Freddie!!

The Mother of Billy and Alice appears at the back.

Mother Billy!!

Alice Mum!!

The fight stops. They pick themselves up.

Freddie *(beaten up)* Here she is. Ask her if you're not going in a home, both of you. You are. Go on – you ask her.

Billy Mum, it's not true, is it?

Alice Mum, say it's not true. Mum!

A pause and Mother turns away.

Alice/Billy Noooooooooooooo.

Their cries echo as The Gang laugh and point and run off.

Alice/Billy Mum!!

The Gang *(echoing)*

O-U-T spells out, so out you must go
Because the King and Queen say so.

Two Young Adults come on.

Adult 1 I'm from the Boys' Home, Billy. You'll be coming with me.

Adult 2   Come on, Alice. You'll like the Girls' Home.

Alice/Billy   Noooo!

The Young Adults each take one of the Simmons kids by the arm and lead them off in opposite directions. They resist as hard as they can.

Alice   Billy!!

Billy   Alice! Alice!!

Scene 8

School playground, today. Lights on Old Billy at the fence.

Old Billy   Alice!!

Charlie and Elizabeth look at him and look again at the documents. They scrabble through some of the other papers.

Charlie   Can't find anything about no children's home.

Elizabeth   *(of a page)* What's this?

They read.

Scene 9

The docks in the 1950s. Slowly bring up the sound of children's marching feet.

A large group of Migrant Children, including the now 14 to 15-year-old Billy and Carole, each with a suitcase, marches on to the stage. There are much younger Children with them. The Children are in two lines and they are marching behind the young and severe Miss Starkey.

Miss Starkey   Keep up, Billy Simmons! Carole Brine, stop talking!

Children continue to march in a circle as Miss

Starkey questions them. They are looking all around them.

Miss Starkey   Now children, does anyone know where we are?

Trevor W   Is this the docks, Miss?

Miss Starkey   Well done, Trevor. And what's this giant thing looming up in front of us?

Jennie   Is that the biggest ship in the world, Miss Starkey?

Miss Starkey   Well I don't know about that, but it is certainly big. Now, can anyone read its name way up there? Who's got good eyes? Yes, Carole Brine.

Carole   The *Orana*, Miss.

Miss Starkey   Nearly. Well done, Carole. The steam ship, *Oriana*. Just a few years ago that ship was bringing our soldiers home from the war. But tomorrow it will be taking all of you children to your new start, your new life in Australia. No. Hand down, child. Hand down, Billy.

Billy   But Miss, I don't want to go to 'Stralia.

Miss Starkey   Australia. Of course you do. It's been decided and it's for your good. Billy, be silent please. Now –

Billy   Miss – the Children's Home said they wouldn't send me anywhere before I could say goodbye to my sister Alice – wherever she's in care.

Miss Starkey   I can't do anything about that, Billy. I have my instructions from the churches, children's homes and local councils who have been responsible for all you children. And they say we're leaving in a few hours.

Billy   Few hours? How can we leave in a few hours? They promised.

Miss Starkey   Well, I'm sorry, I can't help that. Now –

Jennie   Is that Australia over there, Miss?

Miss Starkey   No, Jennie. It's a long way away.

Nan   Miss, does our Mum know we're going to Australia? Has she said we could?

Miss Starkey	I'm sure your mother will be very grateful to know that you are having the chance of a new life in the sun. Oh look! Look, children! One of the crew. They must be preparing everything for our departure.
	A young steward, Ronnie Howard, has come on in white uniform. He looks lost.
Miss Starkey	Hallo there! Steward!!
	As Miss Starkey is turned away, Billy and Carole look at each other. They hesitate for a second. This is their chance. They swiftly get down behind the suitcases that completely mask them from Miss Starkey. Then they carefully crawl on their bellies towards the wings and off, one to each side, while Miss Starkey is talking.
Ronnie	Miss?
Miss Starkey	Good day! Say hello to the steward, children.
Children	Good day, Mr Steward!
Miss Starkey	These children will be your passengers tomorrow.
Ronnie	Oh. *(Starts shaking hands with them.)* Ronnie's the name, kids. Pleased to meet you. I'm a new kid, too. First job. You won't see much of me. I'll be serving the first class passengers. You know. *(Puts his nose in the air conspiratorially. He gets a response.)* I'd sooner be looking after you lot, but there it is. Great country, Australia, they tell me.
Miss Starkey	*(as Ronnie continues to shake more hands)* Now, you're all from different children's homes and orphanages but from tomorrow you'll be together on a voyage which will take many weeks. So I want you all to get to know each other. I'm sure Mr Ronnie will be kind enough to show us where we'll be sleeping. This is a great chance you're all getting and don't you forget that. Whether your parents are dead or simply can't look after you – well, in Australia there are families who do want you. They're waiting for you. In towns where you can

work and better yourselves. A new start. A new
life.

Ronnie   Doesn't that sound good? Eh? Right kids, if you're
ready, walk this way.

*Ronnie does a funny limping walk. The Children all
laugh and copy it.*

Miss Starkey   Thank you, Mr Ronnie. Aren't we lucky? Now
children, pick up your cases and follow Mr Ronnie.

*Miss Starkey starts to exit. The Children carry their
cases.*

*The Children limp off, copying Ronnie. As they reach
the side of the stage, Miss Starkey turns and sees
two cases left behind.*

Miss Starkey   Wait! Wait! Wait! All right! All right! Hands up – who
hasn't picked up their suitcase?

The Children all lift their suitcases and show her.

Miss Starkey   What?

*Miss Starkey moves swiftly to the front stage and
looks at the labels on the suitcases.*

Miss Starkey   Billy Simmons. Carole Brine.

The Children say nothing.

Miss Starkey   Did anyone see them go?

The Children shake their heads.

Miss Starkey   If I find you're lying, there'll be trouble.

*The Children shake their heads. Miss Starkey picks
up the cases.*

Miss Starkey   They are two very bad children. What are they?

Children   Very bad children.

Miss Starkey   Very bad and ungrateful children. No wonder their
mothers didn't want them. *(Moving off)* Well, they'll
soon come running when they're hungry. Oh yes.
But they'll get more than they bargained for, those
two. Quick march!

The Children exit, marching, as lights fade.

Scene 10

*School playground, today. Lights up. Charlie and
Elizabeth reading the papers. They look at each other.*

Charlie   Did they get away?

Then the lights down on them.

Scene 11

Another part of the docks in the 1950s. Billy enters.

Billy   *(in a whisper)* Carole!! Carole, where are you?

Carole   Here!

Billy   Where?

Carole appears from the shadows.

Billy   No good. I walked all the way down there and the
dock gate's locked.

Carole   That way's the same. Nothing but ships. Shh.
What's that?

A flash of a torch.

Billy   Down behind here!!

A young policeman, P.C. Wilson, enters.

P.C. Wilson   I can hear you. Come on! Come out!

*He waits. It is a bluff. He flashes his torch round the
area. He sees nothing and exits.*

Billy   Whew. I'm getting out and finding Alice if it kills me.

Carole   And me – I'm going to find my Mum.

A voice from the dark startles them. They freeze.

Maria   You two! Clear off!

*Maria Santorini and Barbara Court move into the
light.*

Carole Who's that?

Barbara We were here first.

Billy Uh?

Maria That copper wouldn't have come this way if you weren't so noisy. Now, clear off!

Carole Are they sending you away too?

Maria and Barbara nod.

Carole Did they tell you why?

Barbara No. Did they tell you?

Billy Didn't tell us anything at the Children's Home. Just suddenly said – You're going.

Carole You on the *Oriana* too? To Australia?

Barbara Australia? Where's that? No. They're trying to send us to a place called Cananda.

Maria She means Canada.

Barbara Yeah, that. Cananada. On the *SS Montreal*.

Carole Canada? Where's Canada?

Maria They say it's near America.

Carole Oh, America! I want to go to America.

Maria Well, I'm not going to Canada and I'm not going back to that Children's Home. They wanted to cut my hair off. My Mum told them never to do that. I'm going to find my Mum.

Barbara And I'm going to find my little sister. And there's nothing they can do about it.

Carole There is if they catch you.

A ship's horn.

Barbara No there isn't, clever.

Ship's horn again.

Maria The *Montreal*'s sailing without us!!

They hug each other as the ship's horn blows again.

Barbara/ Maria	Hurrah!
	They are lit by the beam of P.C.Wilson's torch.
P.C. Wilson	You two! Come here!
	Billy and Carole, out of the torchlight, hide.
P.C. Wilson	You two little perishers. Know how worried everyone is about you?
Maria	If they were worried they wouldn't send us away.
P.C. Wilson	*(moving in)* You're going for your own good. You're orphans. There are families waiting for you in Canada. They're going to look after you.
Maria	We're not orphans. At least, I'm not. She's not.
P.C. Wilson	Of course you're orphans or they wouldn't be sending you. Now come on.
	Ronnie appears, eating from a bag of fish and chips. P.C.Wilson swings his light.
Ronnie	What's this? You want to arrest these fish and chips, Officer? *(He sees Maria and Barbara.)* Are they lost?
P.C. Wilson	Escaped off the *Montreal*, little perishers.
Ronnie	What – don't they want to go?
Maria/ Barbara	Nooo.
P.C. Wilson	Well, they're going.
Barbara	Can't. The ship's sailed.
P.C. Wilson	We'll see about that.
Ronnie	Have a heart. They look hungry. *(To both)* Have a chip. Is that all right, Constable? Go on. Go on. Take a couple.
	They take some chips and nod, and P.C.Wilson takes them off.
P.C. Wilson	Keep your eyes skinned, Steward, for any more of the perishers. See any – grab 'em.

Scene 12

*Same time. Same place. Ronnie stands eating his
fish and chips and moves front stage and looks out.
He is puzzled by all this.*

Ronnie   Why don't they want to go?

*A female steward, Meg Kelly, comes up behind him
and takes a chip as a ship's horn sounds again.*

Meg   Nice chip. First voyage on the *Oriana*?

Ronnie   First on anything. Is it that obvious? Yeah. Ronnie
Howard.

Meg   Stewardess Meg Kelly. *(They shake hands.)* One
word. The Chief Steward. Don't get on the wrong
side of him.

Ronnie   Thanks. Is it always like this?

Meg   How do you mean?

Ronnie   All those kids. Look! Out there. On the *Montreal*.

Meg   Where you looking?

Ronnie   Lower deck. See 'em? All those little faces. Along
the rail.

Meg   Oh, that. We took three hundred to New Zealand
last year. Dropped off some in Rhodesia on the way.
Poor kids from the cities. Children's homes can't
take any more. But they can't get enough of 'em in
Australia, places like that – as long as they're white.
Families waiting for them.

Ronnie   But they're no more than babies, some of them.
Look at that one there. With the dummy.

Meg   Hey, those bigger kids! Wonder what they're waving
at? There's no one here.

Ronnie   I don't know. Well, we're here.

Ronnie starts waving vigorously. Meg follows.

Ronnie   Look, they've seen us!! See, they're smiling now.
Yeaaah. Byeeeee. Look at the little one. Let's walk

along. Bye kids. Byeeeeee. You'll love it in Canada. You will, I bet you will.

They both exit, still waving. Pause and Billy and Carole emerge. They come down to the front and the Montreal *gives a whistle blast. They give a feeble wave. Then they stop and start to think.*

Carole   Time to go, Billy.

Billy   Yeah. *(Pause)* Carole, we're never going to get off the docks. I've got an idea. That man's on the *Oriana*. He'll look after us.

Carole   You think so?

Billy   Well, I'm starving.

Carole   Me too.

Pause as they consider.

Billy   If we run we can catch up before he finishes those chips.

Carole   Race you.

They run off.

Scene 13

The deck of the Oriana. *Sound of ship's horn. A long long blast. Sound of seagulls.*

The large group of Children without their suitcases, including Betty French, Philip Sims, Nan Brookes and May Scott, walk down to the front.

Miss Starkey enters at the back and pushes on Maria Santorini and Barbara Court and Billy Simmons and Carole Brine. They are crying and holding their bums. They've been beaten.

Miss Starkey   You two didn't want to go to Canada. Very well – you'll come to Australia. Stop blubbing, Maria Santorini. Barbara Court! Any more misbehaviour and there'll be more of the same. And Billy

Simmons and Carole Brine – you are wicked children. Don't think you've heard the last of your little escapade. Because you haven't.

Betty Miss, the ship's pulling away. Can we wave?

Miss Starkey What on earth do you want to wave at the empty docks for?

Nan But can we?

They all look at Miss Starkey. She shakes her head over their silliness.

Miss Starkey You are all silly children. What are you?

Children Silly children.

Miss Starkey Oh, then I suppose so. Wave if you must.

Miss Starkey turns away and the Children start waving. (Through this they move backwards as if we are leaving them behind.)

Maria Bye, Mum. Bye Paul.

Nan Bye, Sandy.

Barbara Bye, Sis.

Philip Bye, Rover. And the puppy.

May Bye, Mum.

Billy Bye, Alice.

Maria Goodbye, England.

The lights fade on them still getting smaller.

Scene 14

First class deck on the Oriana/*Lower deck. Sound of seagulls.*

Lights up on upper level. Ronnie Howard over the audience with a drinks tray.

Ronnie One minute, sir! *(Tries to remember his order)* Two pink gins, two whiskies one with one without, and – what was it? One lime. Oh yeah. A Tom Collins.

Meg Kelly appears in the opposite box, also doing drinks.

Meg Ronnie, I'm running out of ice.

Ronnie I've told the Chief. He's sending for more.

Meg You going ashore in Spain?

Ronnie *(to passenger)* Just coming, sir. Can't. Chief's got me down to work. I'll get ashore in Suez or South Africa, he reckons.

Meg How they treating you on 'A' deck?

Ronnie These first class passengers? *(He pulls a face, then whispers.)* Didn't anyone tell them we put a stop to the slave trade? Back in a minute.

Ronnie exits.

Miss Starkey appears below, walking from the back and looking around.

Miss Starkey *(clapping her hands)* Children!! Children!!

Ronnie appears back in his box again.

Miss Starkey Ah, Mr Ronnie. Have you seen the children? It's time for their lessons.

Ronnie They're already doing them, Miss Starkey. Yeah. Last time I saw them they were all studying books.

Miss Starkey Really? Oh.

Ronnie Coming, sir. *(To Miss Starkey)* Oh yeah.

She looks puzzled and wanders up towards the back. Ronnie laughs to himself at his lie and goes. Meg laughs at Ronnie's obvious lie as she watches Miss Starkey still in view. Ronnie arrives back and leans over the box.

Meg What a battleaxe!

Ronnie Not all her fault. Have you seen her boss? He shouts at her and she shouts at the kids. I heard him. Kids get out of line and she's on the first ship home.

Meg Those Australian families'll make it up to them. Coming, sir! See you later, Ronnie. Here, you think

	she's doing anything for 'em for Christmas?
Ronnie	Wouldn't bet on it. Hmm. We'll be off India then. Have to think about that.
Meg	But there's hundreds of kids! Coming, sir!

Meg goes. Ronnie looks out to sea (over the audience). The Kids arrive furtively and look up and wave.

Children	Ronnie!!
Ronnie	Keep your eyes peeled. She's looking for you. Near the lifeboats.
Maria	How are you today, Ronnie?
Ronnie	Mustn't grumble. Here, you'd better go and do your lessons. Before you go *(Looks around)* Do they give you biscuits in third class?
Children	Biscuits?

They shake their heads.

Betty	Why?
Ronnie	*(He looks around again. Whispers.)* See, these biscuits here *(He brings out a big tin.)* are exclusively for the first class passengers. But now that I look – there's something a bit first class about you nippers. Perhaps my eyes deceive me?
Children	Nooo.
Ronnie	What? You are first class but you just happen to be on the third class deck?
Children	Yeaah.
Ronnie	What, and you haven't had your biscuits?
Children	Noooooo.
Ronnie	You've been deprived of 'em?
Children	Yessssssss.
Ronnie	Well, I don't know what to do. I just don't know what to do about this. Not had your biscuits??
Children	Nooooooooooooo.
Ronnie	Not one?

Children	Noooooooooooo.
Ronnie	Not a single, single, single one?
Children	No!!
Ronnie	Disgraceful! Is there no justice? *(Throws biscuits)* Catch!! Catch! Catch!! *(To the audience)* You lot look first class, some of you. Here. Catch! Catch! Catch! Catch!!

The Children scramble delightedly for the biscuits and catch them.

Then Ronnie looks off-stage.

Ronnie	Scarper!! Go and get your books. Tell her you've been studying all morning. I'll cover for you.
Miss Starkey	*(off)* Children. Children!!
Ronnie	See you tomorrow. One moment, sir!

The Children run off. Miss Starkey enters.

Miss Starkey	Mr Ronnie. *(Looks around)* Mr Ronnie!! I'm sure I saw them. Mr –

Ronnie reappears.

Ronnie	Miss Starkey! I don't believe it! They were just here – looking for you. To do their lessons. My fault entirely. I told them to go that way. Coming, sir! Oh Miss Starkey – would you care for a biscuit? First class issue.
Miss Starkey	Ooooo! How kind!
Ronnie	They're meant for the toffs. But as it's you. . . Excuse fingers.

He thrusts one at her and leaves.

Miss Starkey	*(tasting it)* Mmmmmm. What a nice man. A little common, but very nice. Children!!

Miss Starkey exits.

Scene 15

Below decks on the Oriana. *At night. Sound of big waves crashing.*

Nan Miss, I feel sick.

Lights up on the Children, all lying down, pulling a sheet or blanket round them. These are Billy, Carole, Barbara and Maria, Betty, Philip, Nan and May. Miss Starkey walking around them.

May Nan was sick all over me last night.

Nan I couldn't help it! That storm.

Betty I want to go home.

Philip We're all going to drown.

Miss Starkey Now, stop all this nonsense! You've got your bucket. I can't do anything about the sea. We'll be in the Mediterranean soon.

Carole What's that?

Miss Starkey The sea's much calmer there. I'm turning the lights out now.

Betty Miss, I'm frightened of the dark. Can you leave the door open so we can see the light?

Miss Starkey Don't be silly! Lights out. Goodnight. And no talking.

A door slams. The sound of crying mixes with the storm.

Billy Who's crying?

Barbara It's Nan.

Billy Nan, it's all right. It's going to be all right.

Nan It's not. I'm never going to see my Mum again.

Maria Nan, come on.

Billy 'Course you will, Nan. We all will.

Nan I won't.

Maria Tell her a story, Billy.

Philip	Yeah. Tell her that story again, Billy.
Children	Yeah.
Billy	Not tonight.
Children	Billy!!
Nan	Sorry. I'm going to be –
May	Not on me again! Quick – the bucket.
Billy	Philip, chuck it over!
Nan	*(is sick)* Ughaghh.
May	*(with sick all over her)* Philip! I said bucket!
Philip	Sorry.
	Nan's hand is over her mouth. Some hold their noses.
Philip	Ughh! Look – all that carrot's come up! Ughh!
Betty	And peas – ughh!
Billy	Shut up about carrots and peas!
Betty	And that gristle from the stew!
Carole	Shut up!
Barbara	Ughhh! She smells.
Billy	She can't help it. She's never seen the sea before. Get a cloth and clean her up while I tell you the story.
Maria	Pass over a mug of water for her.
Betty	She smells! She smells all of sick.
Billy	Right, shut up everybody about sick! 'The voyage'.
Betty	I like this one.
Billy	Once upon a time there was some kids. Their country didn't want them and they were put on a big ship with a witch.
Children	Yeah.
Billy	They were all missing their mums or sisters and that. Or their dog.
Philip	Yeah. Rover.

Billy   Some days out at sea they decided they'd creep up on the witch, take her a prisoner and make her walk the plank.

Children   Yeaah.

Billy   They waited till they saw some sharks and that's when they did it. 'Mercy', the witch shouted, 'Mercy!'

Children   'No mercy, witch! Walk the plank. Walk the plank!'

Billy   'Walk, walk, walk.' She walked and the children read out the charges against her.

May   'You never gave us a kiss. You never told us a story.'

Maria   'You never let me wear my hair down, like my Mum liked.'

Barbara   'You never said goodnight properly.'

Betty   'You always turned the light out even if we asked you not to.'

Billy   The sharks were looking up and licking their lips.

Carole   Sharks don't have lips, do they?

Children   Shut up.

Billy   She's at the end of the plank. 'Wooooooooooooooo.'

Children   'Splashhhh.'

Billy   'Goodbye, witch.'

Children   'Gobble, gobble, gobble.'

They all make the sound of sharks and laugh.

Billy   Then a shout from the crow's nest. 'Land ho. Australia.' And when the children got to the shore, who was there but the captain of the Australian cricket team – Mr Don Bradman.

Children   Yeah.

Billy   'Children and Ronnie', Mr Don Bradman said, 'I want you to come to my house straight away.' And he pointed to his Rolls Royce car.

Nan   There wouldn't be room for all of us in his car. And I know who'd be left behind. Just because I smelt of sick.

Maria   Nan! Nan! Nobody's being left behind. Now shut up.

May   Yeah, shh.

Billy   They drove along and suddenly in the jungle there was this lovely English house with roses round the door, like on Ronnie's biscuit tin.

Nan   Oh yeah. And with violets.

Billy   Yeah, violets.

May   And foxgloves.

Barbara And coronations.

Maria   You mean carnations, silly.

Billy   Yeah, and a big lawn. And do you know what was on the lawn?

Carole   This is the best bit.

Billy   On the green lawn was all the Australian team in their white clothes. And alongside them all their mothers and their brothers and sisters. They all held out cake and jelly and pop. The coin was tossed and Mr Bradman said 'You bat.' And the children played cricket and scored 538 for seven declared. And Nan got a century and then Betty bowled the Australians out with her spinners for 36.

Children Yeaaah.

Billy   And then Mr Don Bradman said. 'Because of those people in England who were horrible to you and you're such good cricketers you're all going to stay here with me and my mother and all of my team's mothers.' And he pointed to Arthur Morris' mother, Lindsay Hassatt's mother, Keith Miller's mother, Ray Lindwall's mother and all the others. 'And there's something else we're going to do for you.'

Barbara 'You'll get pocket money every week. At least threepence.'

Philip 'You'll have a dog each to play with.'

Maria 'You'll have a goodnight story every night without fail.'

Betty 'We'll leave the light on for you. And we won't make you eat gristle. You can hide it under your fork if you find any, and there'll be no slaps.'

Nan 'No, there'll be no slaps behind the knee or on the hand and no caning whatsoever.'

Billy Right. And then he said, 'We're going to make sure all the people you miss will be here soon.'

Children Yeah.

Maria 'Yeah and anyone you want killed – like those people at the Children's Home – Miss Milligan – who told you lies and wouldn't let you see your Mum – we'll kill them for you.'

Children Yeah. . .

Billy And the English children all said, 'Three cheers for Mr Don Bradman! Hip Hip.'

Children 'Hurrah!'

Billy 'Hip hip.'

Children 'Hurrah!'

Billy 'Hip hip.'

Children 'Hurrah!'

Billy And they all lived happily ever after.

Silence. Children nod.

Betty That's good.

Philip That's really good.

Billy Nan, you still feel sick?

Nan No. I feel a bit better.

Billy Good. 'Night.

May 'Night, Billy. Thanks.

Maria Shouldn't we say a prayer, Billy?

Billy No. If Jesus let us get taken away we're not saying

	anything to him. *(Pause)* Agreed?
Children	*(pause)* Agreed.
	Silence.
Betty	Ronnie says he's coming to see us again tomorrow if he can.
Maria	I like Ronnie.
Betty	So do I.
Philip	He's smart. That white suit.
Nan	I'm going to marry Ronnie.
Betty	I am, too.
Billy	Sleep.
Children	'Night, Billy.
	Pause. Silence.
Philip	Munch. Munch. Munch.
Billy	I said, sleep. Is that you, Philip?
Philip	I'm a shark. I'm still eating the witch.
	Laughter as the lights go down. Sound of waves against the ship's side for a spell. Then slowly bring up Once in Royal David's City.

Scene 16

Same location. Some weeks later. Lights back up on the Children all asleep. One of them wakes and sees a stocking at the bottom of the bed.

Nan	Worrr. I don't believe it. Worrr.
	Others wake and find their Christmas stockings.
Philip	It says from Father Christmas.
Billy	Father Christmas!! There is no Father Christmas. It's Ronnie. It's Ronnie.
Betty	What do you mean there's not a Father Christmas?

Billy   *(after thought)* What I mean – course it was Father Christmas – but Ronnie must have helped him. How else was he going to get reindeers on the ship?

Betty   Oh. Well that's all right.

Philip   I didn't think we were going to get anything!

Billy   Well you have, haven't you?

Children   Yeah.

Lights down as they search in their stockings.

Scene 17

Same time. First class deck on the Oriana/Lower deck. *Carol fades into* Rudolph the Red-Nosed Reindeer.

Meg appears in the upper box wearing a paper Christmas hat. She has streamers round her and carries a tray of drinks. She looks concerned.

Meg   Ronnie! Ronnie!

Ronnie appears looking very happy. Also with silly hat and a drinks tray.

Ronnie   Coming, sir. Be with you in one second. What a party they've got up there!

Meg   Ronnie!

Ronnie   *(brings up a Christmas cake)* For the kids. What do you think?

Meg   Ronnie, seen the Chief?

Ronnie   No. Why?

Meg   Passengers on your deck. Been complaining about the service on Christmas Eve. He's not pleased.

Ronnie   *(amazed)* I asked Jimmy to cover for me. I only nipped off for half an hour to do something for the kids.

Meg   They're making out to him you spend all your time

	with those kids and they have to wait for their drinks.
Ronnie	Most of the time? I do it in my breaks. They're despicable.
Meg	Chief's still talking to them. Look on his face, he's going to sack you.
Ronnie	What? Oh no. Stranded in Australia with no money? Oh no. . .
Meg	Listen. Listen. Listen. Just tell him you're not having anything more to do with the kids. That and you'll apologize to the passengers. It might work.
Ronnie	Apologize to those stuck-up – *(Looks at the cake.)* What do I do with this?
Meg	Forget the cake.
Ronnie	*(checks watch)* I was going to meet them here now to give them their surprise.
Meg	Listen, Ronnie, it won't help them if you lose your job.
Ronnie	These first class passengers have got everything. What have those kids got?
Meg	That's life. Now get going. I'll deal with the kids. They'll have to be told to stop bothering you, Ronnie. OK?
	Ronnie pauses, nods and exits. Meg exits too. The Children enter at the back cautiously, but laughing. Some have funny party hats made from newspaper. They have a large parcel wrapped in newspaper which is coming undone.
Billy	Who wrapped this present up?
Betty	I did. Me and her. Why?
Billy	Nothing. It's good.
Nan	*(whispering up to the box)* Ronnie. Ronnie. We've got something for you. Happy Christmas.
Billy	Must be working. Don't want to get him into trouble.

We'll come back later.

May   *(pointing up)* Look at the toffs. Those dancing dresses. *(She dances.)*

Philip   And penguin suits. May I have this dance?

Betty   Charmed I'm sure.

They all dance with each other, aping the grown-ups on 'A' deck.

Barbara   Ronnie!

Philip   I'm going to have a suit one day.

Nan   Ronnie!

Maria   And I'm going to have a dress like that. And do my hair like that lady.

Meg enters with her drinks tray.

Meg   Won't be a minute, sir.

Billy   Is Ronnie up there, please?

Barbara   We've got something for him.

Betty   And he's got something for us. Well, he said he might have.

Billy   We don't know. He said he would if he could.

Meg   Listen, you've got to stop bothering Ronnie. All right? He's done what he can for you. But he can't see you any more. Right? And you children shouldn't be on that deck there anyway. You should be down one deck. So go on, down you go, and don't come back.

Barbara   *(as others cry)* But we've got this for him.

Meg   You keep it. Thanks. But you keep it.

Meg goes. A devastated pause. They look at each other. Billy, coldly angry, takes the parcel.

Maria   What are you doing, Billy?

Nan   Not over the side. We could use it.

Barbara   It took hours to wrap that!!

Billy flings the parcel overboard.

Children   Ohhhhhh.

Billy   Come on! You heard her. To our own deck. Get going. Get going, all of you, and stop crying. Stop it. There's nothing to cry about. What do you expect? Don't trust anybody from now on, all right? Nobody.

They all go, some crying. The deck is empty. The dance music continues. Meg comes back and looks down at the empty deck. Ronnie appears. He looks down at the empty deck.

Meg   Chin up, Ronnie.

He nods, hard-faced and hiding his emotions, and disappears.

Meg   Ronnie!

Her head sinks into her hands and Meg leans unhappily on the balcony as she listens to the dance music and chatter of 'A' deck passengers. Then a throaty angry roar comes from her. She starts kicking the balcony and pounding her hands.

Meg   *(to the unseen first class revellers)* Satisfied? Are you satisfied now?

Lights out.

Scene 18

Below decks on the Oriana. *All the Children are under their sheets.*

Philip   Billy, can we have a story?

Billy   No.

May   Oh, Billy.

Nan   Please.

Billy   No.

Nan   But you said –

Billy   I said no.

Children Ohh.

Billy   *(coldly angry)* You want a story. Right. You'll get a story.

              They wait – some still crying.

Billy   Once upon a time –

Children Hurrah.

Billy   There was a boy called Hansel and a girl –

Nan   Oh no.

Billy   Called Gretel.

Barbara   Not that one, Billy. Their Mum and Dad want to kill their own children in that one. No.

Betty   It's cruel. Billy, tell us the one –

Billy   No. This one. Do you want it or not?

Barbara   No.

Betty   No.

Maria   No.

Philip   You're horrible, you.

Billy   Good. Go to sleep.

Scene 19

On deck in dock in Australia. A band playing
Waltzing Matilda. *The sound of the ship's siren. The Migrant Children appear – all with their suitcases. They form up in a line at the back. It is sweltering.*

Miss Starkey Well, children, come and look. There's your new home. Your new country. Australia. What's the matter?

Maria   She's fainting Miss, Nan. It's so boiling.

Philip   He is too, Miss.

Miss Starkey   Hold them up. Come on. Brace up. Don't be babies. Down the gangplank. Quick march.

Maria   But she's fainted, Miss.

Miss Starkey   Come on, we don't want to keep your new families waiting. March.

The Children all march silently. But they stay on stage at one side. Ronnie and Meg appear in full uniform in the boxes, as if looking over the ship's rail.

Meg   Shore leave here I come. Days of it. You ready, Ronnie? What's the matter?

Ronnie   *(pointing)* I don't believe it.

Meg   What?

Ronnie   They said there were going to be families waiting for the kids. Where are they, then?

Meg   Maybe those officials take them in those buses. Same with those monks and nuns.

Ronnie   No. No. No. Look what's painted on the buses. 'Children's Home.' No families at all. No ordinary people. And look at the battleaxe. Nobody's told her, either. It's all been lies.

Meg   Oh look – the kids have seen them. Look at their faces.

Lights on young Billy.

Billy   Alice!!

Lights up on Old Billy at the fence.

Old Billy   Alice!!

Lights off on both and up on Elizabeth and Charlie. They look at each other. Sound of children chanting, as though from a distance.

Chant   O-U-T spells out, so out you must go
Because the King and Queen say so.
Repeat once as it fades.

ACT TWO

Scene 1

School playground, today. Music. The voice of Old Billy, shouting.

Old Billy   Alice!!

Into long echo, mixing with ambulance bell which increases in volume. Flashing lights which reveal Gerry in his Council overalls waving and shouting and moving about.

Gerry   Over here. Over here. He's over here!!

Lights reveal the prone downturned body of Old Billy. His suitcase is broken and empty. There are envelopes and newspaper cuttings strewn all over the stage. Elizabeth and Charlie enter, looking back at the lights.

Elizabeth   What's happened?

Charlie   Oh nooo. Is he dead?

Two young Paramedics enter with a stretcher, almost barging them out of the way.

Paramedic 1   Was it you phoned?

Gerry   Yes. *(Indicates)* I was working top floor of the flats. Looked down –

Paramedic 1   Right. *(To Old Billy)* Sir! Sir!

Charlie   *(looking at the prone Old Billy)* Oh noooo.

Gerry   *(as Paramedics examine Old Billy)* Didn't want to touch him. There's an emergency with the drains over there. I'm not exactly –

Paramedic 1   Did the right thing. Sir! Can you hear me? Sir!

Paramedic 2   He's breathing.

The Paramedics get the stretcher laid out.

Charlie   Billy!

Paramedic 1   You know him?

Charlie   Sort of. Yeah. That's Billy Simmons.

Paramedic 1   Wouldn't know his next of kin?

Elizabeth   Alice. His sister. He's been trying to find her.

Elizabeth starts to gather up some of Billy's scattered material while watching.

Elizabeth   Someone mug him?

Gerry   *(picking up a thick rope)* I saw a couple of young fellas running away.

Elizabeth   *(taking the rope)* I'll kill them!!

Charlie   *(as they start to move Old Billy)* Where you taking him?

Paramedic 2   City Hospital.

Elizabeth   *(of all the papers, etc.)* When he comes round, tell him his stuff's safe.

Paramedic 1   Thanks.

Charlie   Can I go with him?

Paramedic 2   What? Why?

Gerry   They had a talk, him and the old fella. *(To Charlie)* Didn't you?

Charlie nods and Paramedic 2, after a pause, gives a gesture of agreement.

Elizabeth   *(putting money in his pocket)* Get the bus back, Charlie.

Other Students have arrived. Charlie walks alongside the stretcher. Donna, Steve Willis and Marcia watch as it goes.

Scene 2

Same time, same place.

Gerry   I've got to get back to the flats.

Elizabeth, who is picking up some of the scattered papers, nods.

Marcia   *(looking around on floor)* Oh no. Blood.

Donna   Who did it?

Elizabeth   I could guess. Take a real hero to knock that old guy about.

Ambulance siren starts and continues through. Elizabeth and others start to go through the scattered material as Eva enters, and on the other side Sandy with her newspaper bag.

Eva   What happened?

Donna   The poor old nutter.

Elizabeth   He's not a nutter. *(Flicking through a bundle of envelopes as Thomas Swift enters)* And, if he is a nutter, he's entitled to be. Look – letter after letter to his sister – the only family he's got – and all they do is send them back unopened.

Sandy   Can we do anything? You know – like – for him?

Marcia   Yeah?

Steve Willis   Yeah.

Elizabeth   Like what?

Sandy   I don't know.

There is a loud, long groan and Mark, with Darren assisting, staggers in. Mark has a bloody handkerchief over his mouth and is moaning.

Darren   Hey! Stop that ambulance for us!!

Mark   *(incomprehensible)* Aghhhhhh. My teeth. My teeth.

Elizabeth   You've got a nerve, you two – coming back here.

Darren   Uh? What you talking about? Ambulance!!

Elizabeth   You'll be lucky. It's gone.

Darren   Where's the nutter?

Eva   Why? Worried he's dead?

Sandy   You've got the old fella's blood all over you.

Mark   *(incomprehensible because of his teeth)* What you talking about?

Elizabeth   *(of the rope)* Did it with this, did you?? Eh?? Eh??

Elizabeth bashes Mark with the rope.

Mark   Aghhh.

Darren   *(stands and grabs at the rope)* You mad?

Elizabeth   *(another blow)* He beats up the old fella –

Darren   *(stepping in)* Him?

Elizabeth   Who else?

Darren   The old nutter beat *him* up.

Marcia   Yeah, to defend himself from you two!

Darren   *(of Mark)* Did what? He saved him, he did.

Elizabeth   Saved? He's unconscious.

Marcia   *(mocking. Of the rope)* What? Saved him with this?

Mark   *(incomprehensible and waving his arms around)* Aghhhhhhh.

All   Shut up, Marshall!!

Darren   He saved him *from* that.

Elizabeth   Na.

Darren   Look at it!

Elizabeth   Why?

Darren   Just look at it, will you!!

It is opened and a noose falls. Surprise. Confusion.

Marcia   *(hesitant)* So?

Elizabeth   *(of the contents of the suitcase)* You didn't do all this?

Darren   What do you think? Shouting 'Alice' he was. Sounded mad. We were at the chippy. Here's one of your teeth, Mark. Then we saw him. Going mad and throwing all this stuff around. Ughh, still got half a chip on it. 'Alice! Alice!' We walked over. He was holding that. *(Gestures at the rope.)* We were standing there. Then he starts to swing it over the school gate.

Eva   You're lying.

Darren   Ask *him*!

Elizabeth   *(less convinced)* How? He's in an ambulance. And you put him there.

Darren   We did –?? The old nutter'd have done himself in if it wasn't for Mark.

Eva   Uh?

Darren   *(of Mark)* He grabbed him, tried to pull the rope away and next thing – whack!! He might be old but he's strong. I thought it was snowing. It was his teeth. *(Indicating Mark)* Old nutter grabbed the rope back. Nothing else I could do. Picked that up and whacked him.

Elizabeth   I don't believe this. He was – ??

She realizes. Stops. She looks at the rope again. They all look at each other. They believe the story.

Mark   *(incomprehensible)* My teeth.

Darren   What's his mum gonna say? Come on, Mark, we'll have to walk it.

Eva   Don't worry, Marshall. You were ugly when you had teeth. You don't look any different to me.

Darren   Oh, very nice. He'll be in the papers tomorrow. You'll see. Have-a-go hero.

Mark and Darren exit.

Scene 3

Same time, same place. The Students pause as they think and look at the rope. Then Elizabeth starts to collect up and look at the scattered stuff.

Elizabeth   We've got to try and find Alice. *(Picking up a paper)* Must be something. . .

Thomas   Here's a copy of one to Margaret Thatcher.

Eva   He should have saved the stamp.

Thomas   'I've written to nine prime ministers and have had no explanation why you sent the children away.' Signed 'William Simmons'. In brackets, 'British'.

Sandy   *(holding it up)* Look – a little Buckingham Palace. Chalk. All chipped.

Marcia   *(holding another)* Big Ben.

Eva   His little bit of England. All chipped.

Marcia   Here's a cutting of the Queen.

Sandy   *(looking over her shoulder)* That's Sydney. You can see that opera place behind.

Steve Willis   That's Billy. In the crowd.

Marcia   That's never him.

Sandy   Look. He's trying to hand her a letter.

Steve Willis   I wonder if she took it.

Eva   No, she never does.

Pause.

Elizabeth   Alice. Alice. Alice.

Eva   Yeah.

Donna   Forty years. She could be anywhere. Why do you think he's got so depressed? He had no chance.

Steve Willis   And it's a common name.

Eva   Not that common.

Donna   She might not even be called Alice Simmons.

Elizabeth	Donna!
Donna	If she got married!
Steve Willis	Could be dead.
Donna	Yeah.
Eva	Why should she be dead?. She lived through the bombing. She'll only be fifty something. My Great Gran's ninety-one.
Elizabeth	Exactly.
Eva	Look – we want to find out how many Alice Simmonses there are – we can.
Donna	I'm supposed to be going to the Metro.
Eva	No one's stopping you.
Marcia	How?
Donna	Yeah. How?
Eva	Phone books. I can get the lot. My uncle works for Telecom.
Elizabeth	Brilliant. You do that. *(Standing with Thomas, who is still collecting papers)* We'll collect up all this stuff first.
Eva	Right. Who's on?
Sandy	*(goes)* I am. *(Of newspapers she needs to deliver)* When I've finished these. Back in half an hour.
Donna	It sounds dead boring.
Eva	Oh yeah. It will be dead boring. But – if we find Alice – it'll be very very unboring. *(Insistent)* Come on.
	Eva takes off Donna, Steve Willis and Marcia to her house, leaving others looking at the material.
Thomas	What's that?
Elizabeth	Looks like part of a diary.
Thomas	Let's have a look.
Elizabeth	Difficult to read his writing. Just a minute, this is clearer. Something tucked in here. *(Spreads out a large paper.)* Looks like a building plan.

*Bring up sound of Migrant Boys singing as Elizabeth
and Thomas read.*

Scene 4

*Australian desert in the 1950s. Music. The sweating,
cassocked young Christian Brother, Brother James,
with his back to us at the front of the stage with the
building plan. The voice of David Steen is heard off-
stage.*

David *(leading the boys)* Pull, boys, pull.

*Brother James has a stick in his hand which he taps
at his side. It is hot. He folds up the plan and rubs
sweat away. Has knotted handkerchief round head.*

*At the same time three or four sweat-soaked
Migrant Boys, bent in half, come in at the side
dragging by rope a great sandstone block. They
work their way across stage, singing. (All of David's
shouts are for Brother James' benefit.)*

David That's it, boys. Put your back into it, Henry.

*Henry sees Brother James near him and covers his
head as if he is going to be hit.*

*At the back appears a big statue on a plinth, pulled
by a number of Migrant Boys spread out like a fan.
It is a figure of a cassocked monk with his hands
outstretched like Jesus.*

Boys Heave!!

The statue inches forward.

Boys Heave!!

*Two lines of Boys in singlets and shorts and with
handkerchiefs round their necks or heads. These
are Henry Smith, their leader David Steen,
Christopher Morris, Brian York, Alex Young and Billy
Simmons. To the side a single boy, Philip Sims, with*

*a wet sheet over his head. They all watch Brother
James carefully.*

David   Pull, Christopher!!

Boys   Heave!!

David   Come on. Got to get Father Donnelly's statue up top
of the hill by dark.

Boys   Heave!

Brian   *(whisper)* Henry – take it easy.

David   Henry's getting heat-stroke again, Brother.

Billy   Could he work out of the sun, Brother, please?

Brother James taps stick on his side.

Boys   Heave!!!

David   Come on, boys. Right to the top of the hill it goes,
boys. Right to the top.

Brother James slowly exits, still watching them.

Boys   Heave. Heave!

David   Henry, just pretend you're pulling till he's gone.

Henry   OK.

Billy   *(whispering)* Are you all right, Phil?

Boys   Heave!

Philip   *(from underneath the sheet)* Can't breathe, Billy.

Billy   *(first taking a look)* Brother Hitler's heading for the
shade. It's all right.

*Philip slips his head out of the sheet and breathes
deeply.*

David   A couple more pulls, boys, till he's out of sight. Billy?

Billy   Yeah.

David   Henry's neck. Heave.

Billy   Come here, Henry.

Boys   Heave!

Henry   I feel dizzy.

Billy   *(adjusting the protection)* What else you gonna feel,
in 106 degrees and your neck frying?

Boys   Heave!

David   *(looking around to check. To Henry)* Into the shade.
               You too, Phil. *(To the three remaining Boys)* You
               three. Just pretend you're pulling while these two
               have a breather. Brother Hitler won't be able to see
               the statue's not moving from where he is.

               *Philip and Henry come into the shadow of the
               statue as the three Boys pull out the ropes and look
               as if they're pulling.*

Philip   I'm starving.

Billy   *(passing across a slice of bread which was hidden
               under his singlet)* Piss the bed and you'll get no
               breakfast. Try and get to the pot tonight.

Philip   It happens in my sleep!

Christopher We're full up. Yeah. That one baked bean on dry
               bread. Ohhh. Yum. Yum.

David   Henry, you're not telling me you fancy eggs and
               bacon like the Brothers fill their fat faces with.

Brian   Shut up about eggs. Please.

Christopher Eggs.

Billy   Eggs. Lovely scrambled, lovely poached, lovely
               fried.

Alex   Don't.

David   Leave him alone.

Billy   On lovely buttered toast.

Brian   Shut up, Billy.

Alex   Ohhhh. Don't. Haven't had an egg since we got off
               that boat.

Henry   *(of the side of the statue)* What does this say?

David   Em. *(He reads and points.)* Father Donnelly's name.
               Then under it says 'Jesus said "Suffer the little
               children to come unto me"'.

               Pause.

Henry   Jesus doesn't want children to suffer. Why did they
               put that?

David   No, Henry. Suffer just means um. . .

Christopher   Just means 'ask them' or 'tell them' to come unto me. Old fashioned.

Billy   He lets them suffer though, doesn't he, Jesus?

Christopher   He doesn't.

Billy   Yeah, so where's the plagues? Where's the locusts he should be sending down on Brother Hitler and all of them? Like he did to . . . whoever it was – the cruel people in the Bible.

Christopher   Billy, he's watching and writing it all down.

Henry   Hey, Billy. And not Brother Simon. Not a plague on him.

Billy   All right. No. Not Brother Simon. Suffer the little children? They will, the poor little kids who have to come here.

David   *(leaping up)* Heave. Heave, my boys.

Alex   What's happening?

David   *(as they rush to pull out the ropes)* Someone's coming. From the road. Can't see. Sun's too bright. Oh no. Not Father Donnelly. Heave.

Boys   Heave!

David   Pull like you mean it. Again.

Boys   Heave!!

Billy   It's all right – take it easy.

Henry   *(pleased)* Brother Simon!!

Christopher   Who's that behind him?

David   Must have run out of petrol. Yeah, look – that sheep waggon way down the road.

Alex   Cor, she looks like a scarecrow.

                   Enter Brother Simon.

Henry   *(pleased and hugging him round the knee)* Brother Simon!

Scene 5

Same time, same place.

Br. Simon   *(rubbing Henry's hair)* Billy. *(Waves over his shoulder.)* This way, boys. Miss. Billy, take these two young chaps to Brother John at the pump. Enough petrol to get them into town.

This as two tough young Australian farmer's sons, Noel and Murray Roche, enter with a Thin Girl behind carrying empty petrol cans. Brother Simon is looking sympathetically at Henry.

Br. Simon   Right, Billy and Henry then. *(To Noel and Murray as he adjusts Henry's handkerchief)* Follow these two boys. They'll fix you up. Billy, have a word with Brother Anselm. He might find a job for Henry.

Murray   She'll get the petrol, Brother. We'll have a smoke here.

Noel   Yeah. She's a lazy good-for-nothing. *(To her)* Go on – get moving.

Brother Simon is shocked, as are some of the Boys.

Br. Simon   Oh well. Umm.

Noel   *(to the Thin Girl)* Get on with it. We've gotta get those sheep to town, you lazy slut.

Br. Simon   I say!

Billy   *(wary of them)* I'll carry those for you, Miss.

Noel   Hey you. Pommy. I said she can carry 'em.

Br. Simon   Boys. Boys. The girl looks all in. Billy'll do it. Now come and have your smoke.

Billy picks up the cans as Noel and Murray are led off to the shade of the statue. Lights on Billy, Henry and the Thin Girl. Isolate them. (Statue should be masked at this point).

Billy   Right. Henry, you run ahead. Get in the shade.

*Henry goes, and they walk. On the spot. The Thin
Girl is looking intensely at Billy.*

Billy   It's not far, Miss. Your brothers always like that?

Thin Girl   They're not my brothers. Thanks for . . . What are
              you building?

Billy   The Christian Brothers' Home for Children. Two
              years. Two years with our bare hands.

Thin Girl   *(pointing the other way)* Is that the pig shed?

Billy   No, the pigs have got a proper shed. That's ours.

Thin Girl   *(holds her nose)* Ughh.

Billy   Yeah. No lavatory. Most of the little kids are so
              homesick – just keep wetting the bed every night.

              *Billy and the Thin Girl reach the petrol pump and fill
              the cans. As they start back, the Thin Girl bursts into
              tears. Billy stops.*

Billy   What's the matter?

Thin Girl   Look at me!

Billy   I'm looking. What?

Thin Girl   Don't you recognize me, Billy?

Billy   Uh?

Thin Girl   I must look a fright.

              Pause. Billy looks closely at her.

Billy   You're not – Carole? Carole Brine!!

Thin Girl   Oh Billy! Billy!

              She throws herself into his arms.

Thin Girl   I think I'm going mad.

Billy   Is that the family who adopted you? We thought you
              was the lucky one.

Thin Girl   Adopted? I cook and clean and sew and scrub and
              wash for seven of them. And –

Billy   And what? Carole??

Thin Girl   Oh, Billy. Billy!!

She holds him hard.

Music and lights on Elizabeth reading Billy's diary as the cry goes on.

Scene 6

A room in Eva Jupp's house today. Elizabeth and Thomas are sitting looking at Billy's diary. Elizabeth is shaking her head. Across the stage, the group of Phoners.

Donna   *(on phone)* Hello. Does an Alice Simmons live there by any chance?

              Charlie comes in. Elizabeth gets up and grabs him and hugs him as mimed telephone action goes on.

Charlie   Hey!! What you doing, Sis?

Elizabeth Nothing. Nothing. How's Billy?

Charlie   Same. But his lips are moving. Saying 'Alice'.

              Eva comes over with a pile of four phone books under her arm, all marked.

Eva   *(frustrated)* There's 26 A. Simmonses in the local book, 20 more in Preston. Liverpool – loads . . .

Elizabeth We've got to try. Look at this.

              Eva takes Billy's diary and reads slowly. She walks around and whistles. Turns the page.

Donna   Hello. Is there an Alice Simmons at this address, please?

Eva   Poor Carole. What did Billy do? Did he punch their lights out?

              She turns the page. We hear Carole's voice, distant and long drawn-out.

Voice   Billlllllly. Noooooooooooo.

              Music.

Scene 7

Australian desert in the 1950s. Billy dashes forward with Carole hanging on to his singlet, holding hard.

Carole Billy, no!! Don't! Don't!!

Billy I'm going to kill them.

Noel and Murray are smoking. They get up. Billy puts down the petrol and confronts them, fists up. The Migrant Boys are sitting around.

Billy You two!!

Carole Billy, no! *(To the Migrant Boys)* Stop him!

Billy Both of you. And I wish your whole family was here. There's only you two. OK. That'll do.

Noel *(throwing cigarette away)* You're going to do what, pommy?

Murray Yeah. What?

Noel and Murray approach.

Boys Get 'em, Billy!

Carole Billy, no! They'll kill you!!

Billy I'll kill them! Come on.

David *(grabbing him)* Billy!! Billy!! Billy!!

David drags him away and pulls him down.

Billy Get off me. David! Get off me!!

David *(hissing)* Billy, if you're trying to – listen – if you're trying to do something for that girl – think!! You hurt them – yeah? They go away from here, who they going to take it out on?

Billy I'm going to kill them!

David Billy!! Billy!! Think!!

Billy Aghhhhhhhhhhhh.

David Billy!

Billy   Agggghhhhhhhhhh.

          *He stands – flinging off David – shaking his head.
          His hands are down.*

David   *(to Noel and Murray)* Take your petrol and buzz off.

Carole   I'll carry it. Come on. Gotta get back to those sheep.

          She looks at them.

Noel   *(to David)* Aw no, mate. You! *(To Billy)* Big mouth.
          Put your hands up.

Billy   No.

Murray   He said, 'Put your hands up'.

Billy   No.

David   Just go!

Noel/Murray   Fine.

          *Noel grabs the unprotected Billy, while Murray
          thumps and kicks him.*

Carole   Billy!!

Boys   *(moving to intervene)* Nooooooooooooooooooo.

          David stops them.

Boys   Billlllllllllllllly!!

David   Leave it. Leave it.

Carole   Billy. Oh, Billy.

          *Billy is on the ground and Noel and Murray are
          repeatedly kicking him.*

          Lights down as the cry reverberates.

Carole   Billyyyy.

          Music and lights fade on Carole.

Scene 8

*A room in Eva's house, today. Lights up at the same
time on Elizabeth and Charlie. Elizabeth closes the
diary. Elizabeth and Eva turn away. Lights on the
Phoners.*

Steve Willis Hello, is an A. Simmons there, please? Ah, Arthur. No Alice Simmons? Thank you very much. Sorry to bother you. *(As Donna takes phone and dials)* Her Dad's gonna kill her when he sees this bill.

Marcia It's cheap rate.

Steve Willis It's not that cheap.

Donna Hello. Oh no. Is your Mum there? Wait. Wait. *(To the others)* They take hours fetching their Mums. Sweetie, anyone there called Alice? Your name's Alice. How old are you, sweetie? Seven. Look – is your Grandma called Alice by any chance? No. Thank you. Don't bother with your Mum. Thank you very much. *(She puts the phone down.)* It's a waste of time, this.

Sandy *(entering with newspaper shoulder bag)* Elizabeth.

Elizabeth What?

Sandy You found Alice?

All Nooooooooooooo.

Sandy Come on!

Elizabeth What?

Sandy You remember that backpacker? No, you weren't there.

Marcia I do. Australian. He wanted 'Sunnyview', Addison Road. You told him there's no such place.

Sandy But there is! Well there isn't, but – look, I deliver papers to a children's home, right – 'Charlton House'? I go there tonight and he's there – sitting down in front of it. The security bloke's telling him to move but he won't. Says he wants information about his mum. Says his mum was sent to Australia from there. Only it wasn't called Charlton House then. It was called Sunnyview.

Elizabeth Sunnyview?? Wait a minute. *(Gets papers out.)* All those letters that Billy sent. *(Holds one up.)* Look – Alice Simmons, Sunnyview Children's Home.

Sandy	Come on!
Donna	Oh yeah. We'll just get on with the phoning. We're not invited.
Elizabeth	*(grabbing Charlie and running)* Donna!
Donna	What?
All	Shut up!
	Music.

Scene 9

Charlton House Children's Home. Steve O'Neill is sitting in the middle of the stage as three small Children play ball round him.

Child 1	What you doing, Mister?
Steve O'Neill	I'm waiting to see the Matron.
Child 2	She's in there.
Steve O'Neill	I know. But she doesn't want to see me.
Child 2	Why not?
Steve O'Neill	Search me.
Child 3	Why do you want to see her?
Steve O'Neill	Well, when my mum was your age she lived here. Long time ago. Then they sent her away. To Australia. I just want the Matron to tell me why they did it. That's all.
	They are satisfied and drift away looking at him as Security Guard arrives.
Guard	Come on now, Mr O'Neill.
Steve O'Neill	I'm on my way, mate. Soon as I get my mother's papers.
	Elizabeth, Charlie and Sandy have entered. They see what is going on.

Steve O'Neill In case you want to go and look through the files –
my mother's name was Maria Santorini.

Elizabeth What?

Guard *(to the Teenagers)* Can I help you?

Sandy *(thinking quickly)* Um, yeah. Remember me?
Newspapers? There's been a mistake with the
order.

Charlie We're waiting for her.

Guard *(nods and turns back to Steve O'Neill)* Come on, sir.
I know you're a little upset.

Elizabeth and Charlie listen.

Steve O'Neill Why should I be upset? This home only sent my
mother 12000 miles away at nine years old. She was
supposed to be here temporarily. Her mother
always made it clear that she was coming back to
fetch her. And she did come back. Only this place
had already sent little Maria to Canada. Oh, except
she never got to Canada. She fooled them but not
for long. Change of destination. Mate, even the
convicts knew why they were being sent to
Australia. My mum didn't. But upset?

Guard But the Matron doesn't have those records, sir. It's a
long time ago and she can't help you. She suggests
you enquire in Australia.

Steve O'Neill Australia? You think they're any more helpful in
Australia? What do you think I'm doing here??

Guard Well, I'm very sorry about that, sir. But Charlton
House really can't help.

Steve O'Neill Well, somebody had better, mate.

Guard This is private property, sir. And I'm sorry, but you
can't sit there.

Steve O'Neill You watch me.

Guard Then I'm afraid I'll have to call the police.

Security Guard takes out his mobile phone.

Steve O'Neill	The number's nine-nine-nine, mate. We get *The Bill* in Australia.
Guard	I'll give you five minutes.
Steve O'Neill	Suit yourself. I ain't moving.
	The Security Guard goes, and Elizabeth and Charlie move cautiously but excitedly over to Steve O'Neill.
Elizabeth	Your Mum? Maria? The girl on the *Montreal*?'
Steve O'Neill	How do you know – ?
Elizabeth	Never mind. When she was here – at Sunnyview – did she ever mention another little girl – Alice Simmons? It's a matter of life and death.
Steve O'Neill	Alice? No. Sorry.
Charlie	Ohh!
Steve O'Neill	And if you get anything out of this place, you're doing better than me.
Elizabeth	*(a groan)* Listen. She'd have mentioned – a boy on the boat – Billy Simmons.
Steve O'Neill	Billy? Aw yeah. Was his name Simmons? *(Leaping up)* You know Billy? Billy was her best friend. Well until – but he's in Australia somewhere.
Charlie	He's here.
Steve O'Neill	What?? He's what? Where? I got to see him. See, something terrible happened. *(He is looking in his bag for a photo.)* She said things about him. I don't know. She still talks about it. All this time she wanted to apologize to him.
Elizabeth	Apologize? What for?
Steve O'Neill	*(shows a photo.)* That's them together. 1956, I guess. She doesn't remember who took it.
Charlie	Is that a church they're standing in front of?
	Start church music and bring up through next speeches.
Charlie	They look so thin.

Elizabeth   And eyes so dark. They look ill.

Steve O'Neill   Well, the way she told it to me . . .

Scene 10

*A church in Australia, 1956. Lights slowly reveal Billy
and Maria standing apart from each other, both
carrying mop and bucket. Behind Billy is a line of
Boys, behind Maria a line of Girls. To one side
Brother Michael, to the other Sister Mary.*

Br. Michael   Right, boys. You've got until five o'clock to scrub this
church clean as a new pin. Begin. No mess and
remember, God is watching you.

*The Boys move forward, fall to their knees and start
scrubbing*

Sister Mary   My girls will take this side of the church, Brother
Michael. And girls – no talking in God's House.
Begin.

*The Girls come forward, fall to their knees and start
scrubbing.*

Scene 11

Charlton House Children's Home, today.

Steve O'Neill   See, the monastery where they'd put Billy and the
nunnery that took my Mum were only about fifty
miles apart. In Oz that's next door. And every
Saturday they were volunteered to clean the church
for the Sunday service.

Charlie   On the back of the photo. Look. Someone's written
'Christmas 1956 – England.'

Elizabeth   That's Billy's writing.

Steve O'Neill   Yeah. That was their plan.

Charlie   What? An escape? Did they? No, they couldn't have
done . . .

Steve O'Neill looks away.

Steve O'Neill   No. No. It all went wrong.

Scene 12

A church in Australia, 1956.

*(All of Billy and Maria's talk is in whispers. They are
always watching for Brother Michael and Sister Mary
before they speak).*

Billy   Maria? You look terrible.

Br. Michael   No talking!

Pause.

Maria   Billy, it's got to be tonight.

Billy   Maria, I'm still saving. I get paid for the work I do
Sunday in town but Mr Philips keeps the money for
me. We said Christmas.

Maria   I can't wait, Billy.

Sister Mary   Is someone talking?

Henry   *(covering for Billy)* My mop squeaked, Sister.

Billy   Maria, listen, leave it a week. I can maybe get the
money then.

Maria   This morning they thrashed Susan.

Billy   Oh, you didn't stand up for her again?

Maria   Now it's my turn, Billy.

Billy   What are they going to do?

Maria   It doesn't matter but it's now or never. On our walk
back there's a long bend where I can get ahead of
the nuns. They're tired by then and slow. If I can run
west five hundred yards before they reach the bend

they'll never catch me. I'll hide up at the crossroads till sundown. Billy, get ready. I'm going to throw you a map. That's where I'll be. At midnight I'm going to start walking to the coast. If you don't come I'm going on my own.

Billy   I'll be there. She's looking. *(Pause)* OK.

Maria throws the paper. Billy grabs it with his wet cloth and sweeps it under his knees. Sister Mary comes and has a look at the slight commotion down front as Billy and Maria continue to scrub innocently. She looks at Billy and Maria, and then turns away. She inspects the floor. She then claps her hands sharply.

Sister Mary   Right, all of you girls. Rise. In line. Curtsey. Turn. March. *(Saying goodbye)* Brother Michael.

Sister Mary and Girls exit as Boys continue to swab on their knees. Brother Michael comes forward and inspects the floor scrupulously.

Br. Michael   Good. Very good. Now there's one little job to do.

Christopher   I'll do it, Brother Michael.

Br. Michael   It seems there's work to do in the bell tower again.

Philip   *(strangled cry)* Noooo.

Alex   I'll do it, Brother Michael.

Br. Michael   It's the bell again. So the call to the faithful isn't as bright as we would all like it to be.

David/Billy   *(together)* Brother Michael, I volunteer.

Philip   Nooooooooo.

Br. Michael   Ah. A volunteer. Philip.

Billy   *(stepping in front of Philip)* Brother Michael, you know he gets dizzy spells. I'll do it.

Brian   We'll all do it.

Br. Michael   Philip. Up we go, lad.

Billy   Brother!

Br. Michael   *(warning)* A word. A single word.

Philip	Noooooooo. Billy!!
Billy	Sorry, Philip.
Philip	Brother Michael, nooo!!
Br. Michael	Come on.
Philip	I'll tell you a secret, Brother, if you don't make me do it.
Br. Michael	Hmmm?
Philip	Billy's got a note. *(He points)* From Maria.
Br. Michael	What? Brother John! Brother John!!
Philip	Sorry, Billy! Sorry, Billy!
Br. Michael	A note?

Brother John comes in at a lick. Brother Michael gestures and Brother John grabs Billy.

Philip	Billy, I'm sorry! I'm sorry!
Brother John	Be silent, Philip Sims!

Brother John finds the note and hands it to Brother Michael. He reads it. Billy stands stony-faced.

Philip	I'm sorry, Billy.
Br. Michael	Everyone out!

They all get into line.

Br. Michael	Not you, Philip!
Philip	But Brother. I told you a secret. I told you a secret.

Brother John shoves the other Boys away towards the door. Some of them look back.

Philip	Noooooooo.
Br. Michael	Philip.
Philip	Noooooooooooo. I want my Mum!!

Blackout.

Scene 13

The Outback at the crossroads, some hours later.
Maria enters with a small cardboard case.

Maria   Billy!!

Silence. She puts the case down and sits on it. She
talks as though to herself, very quietly.

Maria   I'm coming home, Mum. I don't know how long it'll
take but I'll do it. With Billy I know I'll do it. And you
know how you always said 'Keep your hair that
way. Whatever happens, keep your hair that way' –
well, I have. You were always proud of my hair. I
don't know why but you were. The way you used to
comb it every night? Well, you will again.

A noise behind her. She turns.

Maria   Billy? Thank God. *(Then unsure)* Billy? Billy?

Three torchlights from different directions shine on
her.

Maria   Billy!

We see Sister Mary with two Nuns.

Maria   Aghhhhhh. But nobody saw me. You couldn't have
seen me. Ohhhhhhhhh.

Sister Mary throws down her note to Billy. Amazed,
Maria picks it up and reads. Her face falls even
further.

Maria   Billy, you traitor!! You traitor!! No! No! No!

Sister Mary   The sin of pride, Maria Santorini, is a wicked sin.

The other Nuns grab Maria. Sister Mary takes out a
large pair of scissors.

Maria   Noooooooo.

Sister Mary   You are a disobedient, wilful and evil girl. *(Of her*
hair) You care more for this than obeying God's will.
And you must be punished.

Maria   No! No! No! Mum!!

Sister Mary pulls her hair out and cuts.

Maria   Mummm!!

Lights down on that area and up on. . .

Scene 14

Charlton House Children's Home, today.

Steve O'Neill   They sent her away the next day. And for years she still thought Billy had betrayed her to the nuns. At the same time she knew she must be wrong. He couldn't have. Not Billy. Then quite by accident she ran into a down-and-out panhandling in the street in some country town. It was Philip. He had enough brain left to recognize her. Told her what really happened. Listen, I've got to see Billy and tell him sorry.

Elizabeth is starting to walk off.

Elizabeth   But Billy never could have known what your Mum accused him of.

Steve O'Neill   (*following*) But she knew. She knew.

They exit.

Scene 15

The room in Eva's house, a little later. The floor is covered with phone books as we see Eva with the phone to her ear. She is alone.

Eva   Thank you. Sorry to trouble you.

She dials as Elizabeth, Charlie, Steve O'Neill and Sandy enter.

Elizabeth   Where is everyone?

Eva	Went to MacDonalds – just left. Hallo. I'm trying to trace an Alice Simmons? *(She nods wearily.)* Sorry, wrong number. Sorry to bother you. Thank you very much.
Elizabeth	They coming back?
Eva	*(dialling)* I don't know.
Charlie	I'll take over.

Eva hands him the phone and gets up and stretches.

Elizabeth	This is Steve. His mother was a friend of Billy's.
Steve O'Neill	*(shaking hands)* Hi.
Charlie	Hello. Excuse me. Alice Simmons by any chance? Alicia? Sorry to trouble you. Thank you.

He dials again as Gerry enters, wiping his hands with a rag. His clothes and face are filthy.

Gerry	Any change in the old fella?

They shake their heads as Charlie dials again.

Elizabeth	*(to Steve O'Neill)* This is the guy who saved Billy. Sent for the ambulance. *(To Gerry)* Have you finished over there? The emergency or whatever it was?
Eva	Excuse me, but you smell awful.
Gerry	It's being under people's sinks all day.
Eva	Yeah, well . . .*(Waves her hands)* Worrrr.
Gerry	The Council tenants say exactly the same. Can't blame them, but they seem to forget it's their waste pipes I'm cleaning out.
Charlie	I'm trying to phone.
Elizabeth	Charlie, don't be rude.
Eva	Do you want to come back when you've had a wash?
Gerry	When you're puttying their windows, shaving their doors down – cleanish jobs – I find you've got a chance of a cup of tea from them.

Eva   *(no interest)* How interesting.

Charlie   *(phone in hand)* Oh, Arthur Simmons? No, sorry. Wrong number.

Gerry   *(as Charlie goes on to the next number)* So it's a great surprise – when you're covered in muck – to get offered one.

Elizabeth   I'll get you a cup.

Gerry   No. No. Thanks. That's what I'm saying. Just had a cup – with a lady over there.

Eva   *(ironically)* Oh good.

Charlie   *(phoning)* Hello. Excuse me. Alice Simmons by any chance? Thank you.

                 He looks for another number.

Gerry   Yes. Impeccable place too. Full of flowers. Well, all one flower, oddly enough. Sweet William. Do you know it?

                 Elizabeth and Charlie look at each other. He is clearly a nutter.

Elizabeth/
Charlie   *(completely bored)* No.

Elizabeth   Steve, do you want to –

Gerry   So I'm under her sink and this lady – Mrs Grady – widow woman I'd say – shows me through to the lounge.

Elizabeth   Good. Look –

Gerry   Cup of tea waiting in this room full of lovely flowers.

Elizabeth   *(sarcastic)* Sweet Williams.

Gerry   The only flower she ever buys, she was telling me. When the Sweet William season finishes she puts the vases away till the next year.

Elizabeth   Steve – maybe –

Charlie   Hello. Mr Smith?? Ah. No Simmons there? No Alice Simmons? All right, I only asked. Sorry.

Elizabeth   You'll have to excuse me. I've got to go out to get something for Charlie's tea.

Gerry   *(totally ignoring her)* I didn't notice it at first.

Elizabeth is looking for her coat and not attending at all.

Charlie   *(into phone)* Could you go and get your mum, please? *(To Elizabeth)* Baby's picked up the phone.

Gerry   A photo of a small girl and a small boy. Both in tin hats. You could see bomb damage behind. Brother and sister, you'd be pretty certain. Oh, and in the top corner the first couple of letters of a street sign above them. . . . A. L.

Charlie   Albion Street?

Elizabeth   Sweet William?

Charlie   *(phone down)* Sweet Billy?

Elizabeth   No. You don't mean we've been phoning all over the north of England and – she's been looking down on Albion Street all her life? Well, where Albion Street was?

Gerry   It makes sense, I suppose. Where she and her brother last saw each other. I mean, if it's her.

Elizabeth   Yeah, if it's her she'd have seen Billy at the school gate all day.

Gerry   She was at the hospital today. Her youngest daughter's having her first child.

Charlie   You've asked her if she's Alice Simmons?

Gerry   No. No. *(Takes out piece of paper.)* But I had to take her phone number. In case we have the same problem again. Which we will.

They look at it. Elizabeth flings her arms around Gerry.

Eva   What do we do now?

Elizabeth reaches for the phone and then stops.

Elizabeth   I don't know what to say. What if it's not her?

Charlie I'll do it.

Elizabeth No, wait!

Charlie *(dialling while Elizabeth jitters round the room)* If I say 'Is that Alice?' and she says 'No', we can forget it.

Elizabeth nods and paces.

Charlie Hello. I don't know if I've got the right number. Mrs Grady? Is that Mrs Alice Grady?

He cups the phone. His eyebrows go up. It is clearly an Alice. Elizabeth walks round like a cat on hot bricks.

Elizabeth Let it be her.

In doing this she bumps into all the others – Marcia, Thomas and Donna – who have come back in.

Elizabeth Oh!!

Thomas *(looking at Charlie)* What's happening?

Elizabeth Shhhhhhhhhhhhhh!

Charlie *(on phone)* Alice Simmons that was?

The others gasp. They wait for Charlie's reaction. Charlie almost has a heart attack. He nods his head to Elizabeth. The others gather round.

Charlie Mrs Grady? Me? You don't know me. My name's Charlie. Listen are you standing up? *(Pause)* No. No. It's not bad news. Sorry. No. I'll hold on. Can you pull up a chair and sit down. *(Cups phone)* She's doing it.

Elizabeth Give me that, Charlie.

Gerry He's doing fine.

Donna How did you find her?

Elizabeth *(points to Gerry)* Shh.

Donna *(heavy whisper)* Why didn't you call us? Blooming cheek. We've been phoning all night.

Thomas Donna!

All   Shut up!

Charlie   *(to All)* She's back. *(To phone)* Yes, it is good news. *(Pause)* What? Oh no. No it's not the lottery. *(Cups phone)* She thinks it's the lottery. Mrs Grady, are you still there? *(He cups the phone. He shakes his head. Where has she gone?)* Hello. Yes, I'm still here. *(Longer pause).* She said 'It's about Billy, isn't it?'

              Pause. They look at each other.

All   Yesssss!

              And they hug.

Charlie   She's crying. What do I say now? Sis, what do I say now??

              Young Billy enters from the side downstage, Young Alice from the other side, in a repeat of the wartime scene.

Young Alice   Billy!!

Young Billy   Alice!!

              They reach each other and hug. A Recorded (official-sounding) Voice is heard.

Voice   *(over the long hug)* It was an excellent idea, by and large – the Child Migrant Scheme. Australia, Canada, New Zealand – they wanted bigger populations. And in England there were these thousands of what today you would call street kids. Well, they were going to cause a lot of trouble unless we did something. We gave them the chance of a new life in these young countries. A wonderful life.

              Lights down as Young Billy and Young Alice embrace.

Questions and Explorations

Keeping Track

Act One

Scene 1
1 Where do you think Steve O'Neill has travelled from?
2 Why are Gerry and Millie working in the school grounds?
3 How long has Old Billy been standing at the railings?
4 Why do the schoolchildren react to him as they do?

Scene 2
1 What does Millie find in the hole in the playground?
2 What do you learn about Charlie Carter?

Scene 3
1 Why does Gerry suggest a tea break?
2 What starts the bullying in this scene?
3 What do you learn about Mark Marshall's character?
4 How do others feel about him?
5 What kind of person is Elizabeth?
6 Why can Elizabeth decide where she and Charlie go and what they do?

Scene 4
1 What more do you learn about Old Billy in this scene?
2 What is special about the photograph that Tricia has?
3 How does the play make it possible for the young Alice Simmons to appear at this point?

Scene 5
1 What is happening at the start of this scene?
2 What more do you learn about Alice and Billy?
3 How do the children react to the bomb attack and the war?

Scene 6
1 What is special about the day on which this scene begins?
2 Who are the Tommies?
3 What happens in this scene to make you realize that the end of the war brings both happiness and difficulties? Think about:
   • Billy's response when asked if he can spot his father
   • how the wartime children talk about each other's fathers
   • what you learn about some of the servicemen
   • what happens to the various children.

Scene 7
1 How do Billy, Alice and Carole react to being left?
2 What does the gang tell you about Billy's father?
3 What do you learn about Carole Brine's parents?
4 What does the gang say will happen to Billy, Alice and Carole? Are they right?
5 What different emotions are introduced in this scene? Think about:
   • the attitude of the gang
   • what happens to the relationship between Billy, Alice and Carole
   • what happens at the end of the scene.

Scene 8
1 What is the effect of showing you Old Billy at the fence, calling for Alice, at this point? Do you still think he is 'an old nutter'?

Scene 9
1 Where do the children march to?
2 What do they discover is going to happen to them?
3 What does Billy say to Miss Starkey when he realizes?
4 How does Miss Starkey respond to Billy? Who has decided that the children should go to Australia, and why?
5 What does Nan ask Miss Starkey?
6 What do you think about Miss Starkey's reply?
7 What is Ronnie Howard's job?
8 How does Ronnie behave towards the children?
9 How does this compare with the way Miss Starkey acts towards them?

10 What opportunities does Miss Starkey tell the children Australia will offer?
11 Why are two of the suitcases not picked up?

Scene 10
1 When Charlie and Elizabeth look at each other, what might they be thinking? What do they have in common with Billy and Alice?

Scene 11
1 What are the children trying to do in this scene?
2 What country were Maria and Barbara being sent to?
3 Are Maria and Barbara orphans?
4 How does P.C. Wilson respond to the children?

Scene 12
1 What more do you learn about the Child Migrant Scheme from Meg Kelly?
2 What range of ages are the children?

Scene 13
1 How far does Miss Starkey understand the children?
2 Why do the children wave to the empty docks?

Scene 14
1 What is life like on the First Class Deck?
2 How does Ronnie Howard try to protect the children from Miss Starkey?
3 What does Ronnie say about Miss Starkey that gives you an insight into her behaviour?
4 How does Ronnie try to make life more enjoyable for the children in Third Class?

Scene 15
1 How well are the children coping with the journey?
2 What is the significance of the story that Billy tells to make them feel better?
3 What images of home and Australia do you gain from Billy's story?
4 Why do the children not say their prayers?

Scene 16
1   Why is Christmas important to the story at this moment?

Scene 17
1   What happens to Ronnie?
2   What have the children got for Ronnie?
3   What do the children see on the First Class Deck?
4   What does Meg Kelly tell the children to do?
5   How does this affect Billy and the other children?
6   How does Meg Kelly feel at the end of the scene?

Scene 18
1   In what way has Billy changed?
2   What is the significance of Billy starting the story of Hansel and Gretel?
3   Why do the children not want to hear it?

Scene 19
1   What are the children's first impressions of Australia?
2   Who is waiting for the children in Australia?
3   What do we learn about Miss Starkey?
4   What effect does the situation have on Meg, Ronnie and the children?

Act Two

Scene 1
1   What seems to have happened to Old Billy?

Scene 2
1   What conclusion does Elizabeth jump to?
2   What do you discover from Darren Andrews about what Old Billy has tried to do?
3   What more have you learned about Mark Marshall?

Scene 3
1   What does Elizabeth find?

2 What does Elizabeth decide to do about it?
3 How are the others going to help?

Scene 4
1 What are the migrant boys doing?
2 What happens to Henry Smith?
3 What impression do you receive of Brother James?
4 How do the boys cope with what is happening to them?
5 What is the significance of the inscription under the statue?

Scene 5
1 What impression do you receive of Brother Simon?
2 How do the Australian boys treat the thin girl?
3 What are the migrant boys building?
4 What conditions do they have to live in?
5 What do you find out about the thin girl's identity?
6 How is the girl treated by the Australian family?

Scene 6
1 Why do you think Elizabeth grabs and hugs Charlie?

Scene 7
1 Why does Billy pick a fight with the Australian boys?
2 How does David Steen react?
3 How do the Australian boys treat Billy?

Scene 8
1 What does Sandy tell Elizabeth?
2 How does Elizabeth react?

Scene 9
1 What do Elizabeth, Charlie and Sandy overhear from Steve
   O'Neill's conversation?
2 How does the Children's Home respond to Steve's enquiries?
3 What do Steve and Elizabeth piece together?

Scene 10
1 How are the migrant children treated?

Scene 11
1   What impression do you receive about the attitude of the Church towards the migrant children?

Scene 12
1   How do Maria and Billy communicate?
2   What is Maria's plan?
3   How do the boys support one another?
4   Why does Philip tell Brother Michael about the note?

Scene 13
1   What is important to Maria about her survival so far?
2   Who overhears, and how do they react?
3   How does Maria think they found out about her plan?

Scene 14
1   Why does Steve want to find Billy?

Scene 15
1   What work has Gerry Higgins been doing before he arrives at Eva's house?
2   How does Elizabeth react to Gerry?
3   What has Gerry discovered?
4   How do the contemporary English children solve the mystery?
5   What effect is produced by placing the final statement of the play immediately after Alice and Billy's reunion?
6   What are your thoughts about this statement?

Explorations

A CHARACTERS

1 Draw silhouettes of Billy and Carole. On the outside of each
   silhouette write notes about key events which affect their lives
   and over which they have no control. Inside each silhouette
   write notes about how Billy and Carole react to these events,
   and what makes them the characters they are.
   • What are their hopes and fears?
   • What do they care about?

2 Write notes for the actor playing Billy.
   • What would you expect him to look like?
   • What is the relationship between the younger and older Billy?
   • How should he play the character?
   • What skills does he need and what emotions should he use?

3 Choose three characters who are sent to Australia in the play.
   Write three 'goodbye' letters from them:
   • one to their family
   • one to their friends
   • one to an authority figure.
   Focus on the *differences* between the letters.

4 Imagine what might happen to Billy and Alice following the
   end of the play. Improvise scenes that take place a day, a
   week and a year later. Involve any of the other characters from
   the play.

5 Write a scene which involves Billy and Alice together at
   Christmas and includes one of Billy's stories.

6 Write school reports for two of the present-day characters in
   the play, as if you are their year tutor. Choose two characters
   with different personalities.

7   Choose one of the characters. Write a monologue (speech) in
    which they reflect upon their life.

8   Imagine that you are one of the present-day schoolchildren who
    helped piece together Billy and Alice's story. Write a poem, story
    or song looking back at what Billy has achieved.

B SETTING

Australia fact file
*   Australia is a large country of approximately 4,000km by
    3,200km.
*   It consists of five states: New South Wales, Northern
    Territory, Queensland, South Australia and Western
    Australia.
*   There are different climactic conditions, with an average
    summer temperature above 27 degrees celsius and an
    average winter temperature above 13 degrees celsius.
*   It is a country of immense contrasts. It has more than
    2000 National Parks and many nature reserves and
    wildlife sanctuaries.
*   These include: tropical sanctuaries, rainforest, desert,
    snow-capped mountains, islands, coral reefs, estuaries
    and glacial lakes.

Contrasting countries
Think of all the things you know about England and Australia,
including details given in the play. Brainstorm these on a piece of
paper.

1   How do the countries differ?

2   What might people enjoy or find difficult if they emigrated from
    one country to the other?

Room maps
Imagine that your classroom is a map of England/the world.

1   Stand in the area where you were born. If all the class was born
     in the same area, the room then becomes that town, city or
     county.

2   Where were you living at the ages of 3 and 6? Where do you
     imagine you will be living when you are older?

3   How might you feel if you were forced to move against your
     wishes?

C DRAMA

Freeze
In groups of four, choose moments from scenes in the play involving
at least three characters.

1   One person should be 'director' and mould the other three into a
     position that most effectively shows the attitude of each
     character and what is happening in the scene.

2   When everyone is frozen the director touches each character on
     the shoulder. The chosen character must tell the others how that
     character is feeling.

Objects
Choose one of the objects below and improvise or write a story
about what you find in it:
• a suitcase   • a hole in the ground   • a secret diary.

The Auction Game
In a class of thirty pupils you have five red and twenty-five green
pieces of paper which are distributed among the class.

1   On each of the green pieces of paper is written a list of words
    describing various qualities: patient, happy, shy, talkative, friendly,
    quiet, kind, thoughtful, confident, helpful, capable, inquisitive,
    generous, gentle, cheerful, sensible, serious, polite, honest, careful,
    contented, dependable, reliable, punctual, trustworthy, and so on.

2   All the people who receive green pieces of paper should get into
    pairs and decide which word from the list best describes each of
    you. Write the word on a large piece of paper.

3   The people who receive red pieces of paper get into a small
    group. Decide which qualities would be most useful or cause
    you the most problems if you were choosing a 'slave'.

4   The red pieces of paper indicate buyers and the green pieces of
    paper indicate 'slaves' to be auctioned. Each bidder has £100 and
    must bid for the slaves they want.

5   How did you feel about being treated in this way?

6   How does this exercise help you prepare to play any of the
    characters in the play?

Choose your future

Many characters in the play find their lives affected by outside events
and decisions other people make for them. Yet they also have choices
to make which affect their own future directions. In small groups:

1   Find any moment in the play when a character is faced with a
    choice (either their own or one that affects them).

2   Act out the moments immediately before the choice, stopping
    the action at the point where a decision needs to be made.

3   Two members of the group play 'devil' and 'angel' and give
    advice to the character about what they should do.

4   Improvise what might happen if a completely different set of
    decisions are made from those actually made in the play.

D THEMES

Bullying
A number of characters in the play are bullied or abused.

1 Trace what happens in the play and notice the different types of
   bullying or abuse that occur.

2 In your opinion, what is the worst abuse?

3 Create a bullying-prevention scheme for your school. Include
   plans for raising awareness among students and staff and
   suggest long-term measures for eradicating bullying
   altogether.

The right to choose
Many of the characters in the play find their lives dramatically
changed without any choice. What are your expectations of life?

1 In small groups, discuss and each of you note down the order in
   which you would place the following:
   • I buy a car
   • I get married
   • I get my first wage packet
   • I become a grandparent
   • My eldest child starts school
   • I get engaged
   • I retire
   • I become a parent
   • I 'come of age'
   • My children are all grown up and leave school.

2 In pairs, discuss what the next stages in your life might be. Then
   write a letter to a friend about your expectations of leaving
   school and starting your first job.

3 How would you feel if you were Billy or one of the others who
   suddenly had their lives changed by other people's decisions?

Children's rights
In 1959 the United Nations presented the *Declaration of the Rights of the Child* so that governments could make new laws or enforce existing laws enabling each child to have the following:
- the right to an identity
- the right not to be discriminated against
- the right to equal treatment
- the right to family life and education
- the right not to be abused or exploited.

United Nation Declarations of the Rights of the Child
1 The enjoyment of the rights mentioned, without any exception whatsoever, regardless of race, colour, sex, religion or nationality.
2 Special protection, opportunities and facilities to enable them to develop in a healthy and normal manner, in freedom and dignity.
3 A name and nationality.
4 Social security, including adequate nutrition, housing, recreation and medical services.
5 Special treatment, education and care if handicapped.
6 Love and understanding and an atmosphere of affection and security, in the care and under the responsibility of their parents whenever possible.
7 Free education and recreation and equal opportunity to develop their individual abilities.
8 Prompt protection and relief in times of disaster.
9 Protection against all forms of neglect, cruelty and exploitation.
10 Protection from any form of racial, religious or other discrimination, and an upbringing in a spirit of peace and universal brotherhood.

---

1   What rights are Billy and the others denied?

2   What are rights for?

3   Why do we have them?

4 Who gives them to us?

5 Where do we get them?

6 Have you ever given anyone rights?

7 Who decides if you have them or not?

8 Are there some rights that some people do not have? What are they, and who does not have them?

9 If you knew of someone who had had their rights taken away from them, is there anything you could do to change the situation?

E POSTERS

1 Imagine that you are an artist working in Australia. Draw a poster to attract people from England to come and work. Your poster might include:
   • how miserable your home country is
   • how attractive a regular job is
   • the climate
   • what you could do with the money you earn.

2 Imagine that you are an artist employed by the Child Migrants Trust in Britain. You are worried about the hardships suffered by the children being sent to Australia. You have been asked to draw a poster that will show the reality. Your poster might include the following:
   • it is too hot
   • the hours of work are too long
   • there is little food
   • the housing is poor
   • children are the targets of abuse.

3 Find moments from the play that best illustrate each of the ideas you have included in your poster for the Child Migrants Trust.

F THE TRIAL

Child Migration Scheme: what do you think?
Read the following extracts from *Lost Children of the Empire* by
Philip Bean and Joy Melville.

'Who wants to go to Australia? Me! Me! We shouted, putting our
hands up in the air. We thought it was an outing and we didn't
go on many outings.' 10-year-old.

'The nuns at the orphanage told me I was going to Australia.
It sounded great; a land overflowing with milk and honey!'
13-year-old.

The book tells of an era in British history known as 'Britain's Child
Migration Scheme.' Lasting more than 350 years, the scheme did not
end until 1967, by which time 150,000 children had been sent to
different part of the British Empire, including Australia.

Child migration was meant to be in the best interests of the
child. But throughout its history, the children never came first.

'Coming to Australia', said a child migrant, 'was like coming
from the warmth to the cold. I'll never forget. Why did they do
it?'

1   Was child migration a good or a bad idea?

2   Why did it happen?

3   Should it have been stopped?

4   How did people change?

5   What about the rights of each of the individuals?

6   Using evidence from the play, draw up lists of points for and
    against the scheme.

For	Evidence	Against	Evidence

7   Divide into groups (imaginary or taken from the play) of:
    • parents
    • organizers
    • children.
    Improvise possible reasons why the children need to be sent
    away.

8   Now improvise possible reasons why the children should stay.

9   In small groups, discuss what you think about the evidence
    presented. Which side of the argument does your group support?
    Report back to the class.